'The psalmist says that God'. [...]
Miranda Threlfall-Holmes wri[...]
God's word, found it to be go[...]
wants us to eat as well. She in[...] [...] of discovery; the delights and challeng[...] [...]ple as food for
the journey of life. Lots of books [...]ll us what the Bible is
about. Few explain to us how to read it. But drawing on different traditions of reflective biblical reading, Miranda gives us
the confidence to sit and taste its profound and life-changing
goodness.'

Stephen Cottrell, Archbishop of York

'To me, the Bible is one of the most beautiful and dangerous texts in the world – beautiful because it points towards
unimaginable glories, dangerous because it is so easily used as
a weapon to judge, condemn, harm. We need wise companions like Miranda Threlfall-Holmes to help us find the Bible's
beauty while refusing to weaponise it. There's really no book
like *How to Eat Bread* – honest about the Bible's challenges,
inspired by its wonders, informed about its scholarship and full
of practical ideas for reading the Bible as you would eat good
bread.'

Brian D. McLaren, author of *Faith After Doubt*

'The Bible is a beautiful, inspired, ancient sacred text. It's full
of God's wisdom and nourishment – but frankly it can also
be confusing and indigestible without a guide. In *How to Eat
Bread* Miranda guides us to read well, and through reading to
live well, as we come to taste the wonderful food that God
gives us through Scripture. Highly recommended!'

Paul Bayes, Bishop of Liverpool

'For any Christian – or, we might argue, anyone wanting to have even a cursory understanding of how our globalised world got to think and be as it does and is – reading the Bible ought to be as natural as breathing or, as this exciting new book puts it, eating bread. All too often reading the Bible can seem – even to Christians – a scary or taxing task. In this exhilarating and hands-on book Miranda Threlfall-Holmes provides a fantastic guide to the many and varied ways that we can get real nourishment out of Scripture. The Church is in great need of ways to re-engage people with the joys and challenges that reading the Bible can bring and – whether it is for a set group or just the curious individual reader – this marvellous book is a fantastic starting point for that process to begin.'

Fergus Butler-Gallie, author of *A Field Guide to the English Clergy*

'Are you baffled by the Bible, stumped by the Scriptures? Try Miranda Threlfall-Holmes's new book for help. *How to Eat Bread* provides many different ways of tasting the word of God. No need to read it all in one go. Just dip into it, alone or with a group. Miranda Threlfall-Holmes draws on her wide experience in parishes, as university chaplain and as mother, to suggest various ways of reading the Scriptures, suitable for different persons and for different times. Try them. You will not be disappointed.'

Cardinal Michael Fitzgerald

'Miranda Threlfall-Holmes writes with a freshness and an urgency that draws the reader into her subject matter in compelling ways. *How to Eat Bread* discusses in accessible form Scripture's own methods of interpreting the story of God's engagement with creation, the Church's interpretations across history together with the ways in which modern hermeneutical scholarship discloses the inherited texts and their freshness for successive generations. Whether you are beginning this journey or are a seasoned campaigner, you will find something here to enrich your understanding and enjoyment of Scripture.'

Michael Jackson, Archbishop of Dublin

'Miranda Threlfall-Holmes's latest book is a feast of delicious morsels. *How to Eat Bread* is an invitation to read the Bible as a staple of our spiritual life, and yet more: the book is infused with a passion that dares to wrestle with the Bible's trickier aspects as well as its sublime simplicity. In a book that will feed both individuals and groups, Threlfall-Holmes wears her learning lightly. By daring to knead Scripture into the insights of tradition and reason, she has produced a "recipe book" for anyone wanting to discover why the Bible is the greatest companion on the way to God. Taste, eat, and be fed!'

Canon Rachel Mann, priest, scholar and author

'Reading Revd Dr Miranda Threlfall-Holmes's *How to Eat Bread*, I discovered the practical guide to reading the Bible I did not realise was missing in my life. Even with nearly forty years' studying the Bible, she revealed to me new insights, techniques, and doorways for engaging the Scriptures.'

Peterson Toscano, LGBTQ human rights campaigner and creator of Transfigurations – Transgressing Gender in the Bible

'You can't understand what motivates millions of people around the world, or a lot of history and contemporary politics, if you don't delve into the Bible, and grasp something of its complexity. This book offers a rich diet to feast upon: accessible, witty, insightful and wise. You will be stimulated, surprised, and hopefully changed by reading and digesting its contents.'

Helen-Ann Hartley, Bishop of Ripon

How to Eat Bread

21 Nourishing Ways to Read the Bible

MIRANDA THRELFALL-HOLMES

HODDER &
STOUGHTON

First published in Great Britain in 2021 by Hodder & Stoughton
An Hachette UK company

1

Copyright © Miranda Threlfall-Holmes, 2021
A CIP catalogue record for this title is available from the British Library

Trade Paperback ISBN 978 1 529 36447 7
eBook ISBN 978 1 529 36449 1

Typeset in Monotype Bembo by Manipal Technologies Limited

Printed and bound in Great Britain by Clays Ltd, Elcograf S.p.A.

Hodder & Stoughton policy is to use papers that are natural, renewable and recyclable
products and made from wood grown in sustainable forests. The logging and
manufacturing processes are expected to conform to the environmental regulations of
the country of origin.

Hodder & Stoughton Ltd
Carmelite House
50 Victoria Embankment
London EC4Y 0DZ

www.hodderfaith.com

For Phil, and for St Bride's

Contents

PART THREE: Molecular gastronomy – reason

Introduction

You might have various questions as you hold this book in your hands.

Perhaps you wonder why on earth anyone would bother to read the Bible at all. Isn't it a dead book, of only antiquarian or academic interest? Why on earth would a reasonably intelligent modern-day person take more than a passing interest in what it has to say?

Or perhaps your questions are very different. Does it seem totally obvious that one should read the Bible, but you're bemused by the idea that there could be more than one way of doing so? Doesn't the Bible say it, so we should believe it?

Or you may be intrigued but perhaps rather intimidated. The idea of reading the Bible is something that attracts you and you've found that it's not as simple or as one-dimensional as it is sometimes presented, but twenty-one different ways? Really?

I hope this introduction will address these questions. But first, perhaps the most obvious question of all: why on earth call this book 'How to Eat Bread'?

The title draws on several different reference points. It pays tribute to Henri Nouwen's phrase 'bread for the journey', which in turn was inspired by the insight of medieval theologians that the Bible is meant to be nourishing. Less spiritually, the title is also inspired, in part, by Nigella Lawson's 1998 cookbook *How to Eat*. Lawson's book turned cookery writing on its head. She shifted the focus of a cookbook from the proficient accomplishment of cookery techniques, taught by a trained chef, to the enjoyment of eating, taught by someone who loved to eat. In a similar vein, this isn't a technical guide to the art and science of biblical interpretation by a specialist Bible scholar; rather, it's a handbook on how you can be nourished in your faith by reading the Bible, by someone who has found nourishment there herself.

Bread is simple. It's a nourishing, portable, basic foodstuff that is different in and yet common to a very wide variety of global cuisines. Bread is a symbol for many of us of home comforts, of providing for our families, of safety and security. It's notable that in the first Covid-19 lockdown of 2020, bread flour and yeast quickly sold out, as people stayed home and addressed their anxieties by the comforting practice of baking bread. But simple as bread is, it comes in an almost infinite variety of types, some more challenging to bake than others. Sourdough, flat breads, enriched doughs, gluten free … the simplest combination of basic ingredients can occupy bakers for a lifetime.

The Bible, this metaphorical bread for our spiritual journey, is also on the one hand simple and on the other bafflingly complex. It's a book, an anthology of shorter books, containing some of the best-loved and well-known stories that our culture has seen. Noah's ark; the Good Samaritan; Christmas. Simple stuff, retold to children in endless picture books and cartoons and soft toys. But at the same time anyone who has ever picked up the Bible and tried to read through it starting at the beginning will know that it is not simple at all. It lulls you into a false sense of security at first, with familiar landmarks like the Garden of Eden, only to have you bogged down in bewilderment some pages later as the body count and obscure ancient laws and regulations mount up around you.

Why read the Bible?

So why should you bother to read the Bible at all? Why not just follow Jesus and try to be a good person? Or why do you need any help or particular ways to read it – isn't it just obvious what it says, and all we are called to do is obey it?

Here, in no particular order (as they say on the talent shows) are my top reasons for reading the Bible – the whole Bible, not just the bits we like– and for thinking about how we read it.

Jesus thought reading the Scriptures was important

Jesus frequently referred to 'the Scriptures', meaning what we call the Old Testament or Hebrew Scriptures (obviously, what we call the New Testament didn't exist in Jesus' lifetime). He clearly thought they were important, quoted them, and referred to himself as fulfilling them. And the sayings of Jesus that are collected for us in the Gospels are the bits of what he said and did that the early church thought were important. That means that the first generations of Christians thought that Jesus' references to the value of the Scriptures and the law were important enough to pass on. We can't fully understand the Gospels and New Testament letters, or what the early church mindset was like, without having an appreciation of the main elements of the Old Testament. It's just not coherent to say, as I sometimes hear, that we can follow Jesus but we're not interested in the God of the Old Testament.

Reading the Bible is nourishing

Bible reading feeds the soul in a way that is widely experienced as different in quality from the nourishment we get from reading other kinds of books, even spiritual books, and from doing other kinds of activities, even religious practices. The Bible – a collection of sixty-six different books, several of them themselves containing material brought together over time – has been collected and shaped over thousands of years, not as an academic exercise but as the fruit of collective experience. These are the books, the stories, the poems and the memories that many people have experienced as nourishing in this soul-deep way. They're not simply a list of beliefs about God that are meant to be agreed with. Some of them are stories, thought experiments or dreams that are meant to be troubling, unsettling, or even to make you angry. They are food for thought, in the deepest sense. Even if they seem odd, distant or troubling to us now, it is worth reading them and trying to discover what it is about them that has caught people's imaginations and meant that *these* are the stories that couldn't be left out.

Reading the Bible helps us to understand and appreciate our culture and history better

The Bible is foundational for so much of contemporary human culture that not knowing it well means we miss out. Vast amounts of art, literature and thought systems, from cultures around the world, are based on or make reference to stories, characters and debates from the Bible. If you don't read the Bible for yourself it can be easy to miss these references and not realise some of their subtleties and implications. This is true not only of church culture and belief, but even for many aspects of the modern secular worldview, such as humanism, which are deeply rooted in Christian understanding even as they reject it.

Reading the Bible protects us from its misuse

Religion, like politics, is clearly not immune to being manipulated in the service of powerful interests. Reading the Bible and knowing the stories it contains helps us understand and appreciate the nuances of a lot of political and ethical debate. It helps us to be more alert to when people are using biblical references either ignorantly or dishonestly to manipulate public feeling.

Reading the Bible in many different ways is an essential part of the Christian tradition

For two thousand years Christians have read, discussed and thought about the biblical texts, while for many thousands of years more, Jews have read, discussed and thought about the Scriptures that we share. They have shown a remarkable variety of ways of reading and interpreting them that we tend to forget in our contemporary world, when we are too ready to consign everything that is pre-modern to a 'primitive' or 'medieval' past. I quite often come across people who assume that everyone before the Enlightenment read the Bible totally literally and assumed that every word of it was factually true. This is simply not the case, and it can be hugely illuminating to become aware of the many and varied ways that our ancestors understood, appreciated and used the biblical texts. Let's know our own spiritual history, not make the mistake of despising it just because it is in the past.

The biblical texts themselves demonstrate and model many different ways of and reasons for reading other bits of itself

The Bible wasn't written at one time, so when a later part of it was written, the writer(s) already knew about earlier parts and often refer to them, both implicitly and explicitly. The ways in which later books of the Bible quote, redefine and use parts of what was already considered Scripture demonstrates for us a range of approaches that the Bible itself considers legitimate and spiritually useful.

Playing and experimenting with reading the Bible are great ways to learn from experience

Human beings learn best by experimentation and by play. Learning is often equated nowadays with being 'academic', but you only have to watch small children playing for a short while to appreciate just how much the human mind constantly seeks out and desires to make new connections and to learn from new experiences through playful experimentation. Small children learn by handling objects, putting them in their mouths, banging them together to see what happens, role playing different characters and making endless mistakes and discoveries. They learn language by being immersed in it, not by being taught it. And this is how we learn faith – by being immersed in it. We enter into its practices even when they are a mystery to us, and as we surround ourselves with the babble of religious language and concepts, some sort of sense begins to emerge, until we begin to try out the newly familiar words and concepts for ourselves. Reading the Bible, especially as part of a faith community becoming our playmates, is an immersive learning experience that continues to create us throughout our lives. Experimenting with reading it, playing with it, is the best way we know as humans to find our way around it and to inhabit it as our native language and culture.

Who am I?

But perhaps your question is rather different. Perhaps it's more like the one that's going round in my head as I write this: Who is she to tell me how to read the Bible? Or: Who am I to think I can read the Bible rather than just believe what those who know more than I do tell me it says?

These are questions well known to anyone audacious enough to think they might be able to add anything to people's experience of the Bible. They go round in my head, and I guess the heads of all preachers, when we stand up to give a sermon in church on Sunday. They're also questions that I know most of the people I read the Bible with struggle over, even when they're just reading it for themselves. There is something about being confronted with a text that is labelled 'holy' and described as the Word of God, that is pretty paralysing. Who am I, we ask ourselves, to dare to have a view about this text that I'm reading?

So I want to answer this question in two parts: first I'll give you my 'credentials', such as they are, for writing this book for you; and second, I'll talk about why I think all of us, whoever we are, can dare to read the Bible and take seriously our own reactions, opinions and responses to what we read.

I've already mentioned that I'm a preacher. More specifically, I'm a priest in the Church of England, and Rector of three churches in Liverpool city centre. Before I came here to Liverpool, I was vicar of two churches in Durham, and worked in Durham University. I started my ministry in the city suburbs of Newcastle-upon-Tyne, and I became a Christian while I was a student. All of which is to say that I've preached and read the Bible and practised Christianity in a wide variety of contexts and with a wide variety of people.

In my current parish context, we are trying to overturn the assumption that 'the vicar knows best'. We explore the Bible together in services, where instead of sitting in rows listening to the experts, we sit in a circle to remind ourselves that every voice is welcome to contribute and is equal in esteem. In the Covid-19 pandemic, as I write this, we are meeting live on social media every morning to pray, to read through the Bible and discuss it in the comments. We are puzzling out together the passages that seem alien to our current experience, and marvelling at passages that might have seemed alien in the past but seem now to speak afresh. Yet I'm aware that many people feel underequipped to contribute on equal terms. People often ask me for books to read, for courses to study, for Bible classes online and in person, and for ways to find out more. This book is in part a response to that hunger for learning.

I'm also a historian. Before I was ordained, I carried out research and I've taught history both to undergraduates and for ordination and reader training courses in the Church of England. My particular interest is in medieval history, and I love exploring with people the riches of the medieval worldview and its approaches to faith. The central section of this book is a reflection of this, bringing to you the insights and complexities of some of the ways in which the Bible has been read historically, that have been mainly forgotten nowadays except by academic specialists.

In my personal life, I'm mum to three children and I'm passionate about ensuring that children and young people are taken seriously in the heart of church life. My approach to how we learn from experience is formed by my experiences as a mother as well as in universities and theological education. I've greatly enjoyed being trained in and delivering Godly Play and Messy Church, for adults as well as for children. While we were in Durham I worked with my eldest son, and later our local youth group, to explore different ways of praying, and we published these ideas and the young people's responses in *The Teenage Prayer Experiment Notebook*. This has since become a family of books for different age groups, from children to adults. That experience of exploring prayer together, creatively and experientially, has been important for me in developing the ideas that have led to this book. I am more and more convinced that our faith is not something we primarily *learn about*; it's something that we primarily *experience*. Or, to put it another way, I believe that we learn our faith best – as Jesus' first disciples did – by entering into experience first. Defining what that experience 'means' is a secondary activity.

Which takes us on to our second question.

Who are you?

Reading any text is always something of a conversation between the author and the reader. This starts with what books we choose to read in the first place, deciding for ourselves – from the cover, blurb, recommendations and reviews, or from flicking through a few pages – whether this is a book that we want to allow to take up residence in our imaginations. I'm a complete wuss when it comes to violence and horror, for example, but I love classic crime fiction, so my decision-making when I pick up a new whodunnit is a complicated dance between everything from the typeface used for the title, to a quick Google of reviews, to decide whether I am going to enjoy the ride or have nightmares for weeks. We choose with care who we let into the intimate spaces of our living rooms, our beds and our brains.

But even when we have decided what to read, the act of reading itself is not simply a question of downloading the information contained between the covers of the book into our memory banks. Different people will bring different life experiences, questions and assumptions to any text. Whenever we say, on seeing a film or TV adaptation of a favourite book, 'But that character (or place, or tone of voice) is totally different from how I imagined them!', we reveal that we have brought our own imagination to the reading of the book. The act of reading creates something new in our brains – our construction of the characters, scenes and emotions involved – that is a collaboration between the words on the page and our own character, experiences and context. This is true even if what we are reading involves less imagination (a textbook, perhaps, or an instruction manual for a new appliance). We make connections and leaps in logic as we read, because of our previous experience of the subject or of similar literature. It's much easier to decipher the instructions on your second piece of flat-pack furniture than it was for your first.

Give two people the same novel, newspaper article or textbook chapter to read, and then ask them to summarise the key points, and you will never get exactly the same response. Each of us will notice different things in whatever we read. Something in the text might jump out at us because of a connection with a subject that is particularly important to us at the time, or because we have a particularly strong emotional response to it, or already know more about a particular subject. Reading is active, not passive: we cooperate with the author, or the text, to co-create a new reality out of what both parties bring to the reading.

Is this true of the Bible as well? I think the answer has to be yes, because this is what happens when we read anything. Just as Jesus was received very differently by the different people he encountered in his lifetime – some became his disciples, some wanted to kill him or run him out of town – the various biblical texts are received and heard differently by different people. I don't think it's possible to read anything – or indeed meet anyone – and for this not to happen.

This is not to suggest, of course, that the Bible can say whatever you want it to say. It's not that we just find in its pages what we want to see. A conversation always has two or more partners, and not necessarily equal ones. The words on the page matter and our response is to those words, not to a random collection of letters. When we read the Bible, we read the actual text, and our reading is a collaboration with God in bringing our own experiences and contexts into conversation with the text.

Furthermore, the act of reading is never neutral. Do you remember writing up scientific experiments in school, and having to describe everything you did in the third person and passively, as if the experiment had taken place without being touched by human hand ('A test tube was heated' rather than 'I heated a test tube', etc.)? In the Western academic tradition, we have built up a myth of the impartial observer whose reading and experience is taken to be normative. More recently, this has begun to be critiqued; we have become more aware that the supposedly 'neutral' experience is almost always, in fact, assumed to be a male one. It is, moreover, taken for granted that the said male is white, socially privileged, educated, physically mature and healthy, neurotypical, straight, cisgendered ... the list goes on. Until very recently this tacit bias wasn't even questioned, but simply assumed and still is, very often. Fiction is labelled as 'women's' fiction or 'gay' fiction or 'black' fiction ... or simply 'fiction'. No bookshop that I've ever seen has a shelf labelled 'straight white male fiction' because that's just the norm. Similarly, it's only recently that we have become more aware of how much certain attitudes have been taken for granted in reading the Bible. This isn't to say that such attitudes are wrong (there's nothing wrong with being an educated white straight man), but it is important for us to be aware that that set of experiences is not universal; nor should it be considered as normative or be privileged above other perspectives.

So it is important to be conscious of who you are, and what you bring to your reading. Indeed, who you are *is* what you bring to your reading – and means that your act of reading is important and valid. If you believe, as I do, that God made you and loves you and wants a relationship with you, then take that idea a step further, and realise that a relationship is inevitably different with each person. You being you doesn't change God, but it does mean that the relationship you have with God will be different from the one I have.

There are technical pieces of knowledge about the Bible that are helpful to have for some types of reading, and we'll look at several throughout this book. For much of it, though, the emphasis is on noticing how you – and I mean *you*, not a fictional bland objective observer – respond to the text. Because it is in that conversation, that connection, between you and your reality and the reality of the text, that reading happens.

And if this all seems worryingly heretical to you, then I invite you to begin with the first section of this book. This looks at some of the many ways that the Scriptures themselves model and demonstrate different ways of reading the Bible, several of which are clear that the hearer brings something to the story.

Scripture, tradition, reason

This book is divided into three sections, introducing insights and ideas from Scripture, tradition and reason. It's been common in the Anglican tradition to think of these three as the three legs of a stool, supporting and upholding a stable, balanced theology and spirituality. This idea was first clearly articulated by the Elizabethan theologian Richard Hooker, and was popularised in the ecumenical debates of the nineteenth century. At that point, the Church of England, and the other members of the family of churches that it had established throughout the then British Empire, were trying to put into words what was distinctive about Anglicanism as compared to, say, Roman Catholicism or Methodism. The stool idea encapsulated their view that the Anglican Church had a particular stability and structural strength. At the same time, notice the implicit accusation that all other churches were unbalanced! This is a complex image that has considerable overtones of imperialism and arrogance despite its apparent humility and simplicity. Using it while bearing this history in mind shows something of how we can handle the historical complexity of the Bible itself.

The idea is that Scripture (what's written in the Bible), tradition (what's been taught by the Church) and reason (what we can work out by our own rational thought processes from observing the world) are the three sources of authority in determining what is to be believed. In Methodism, this idea is expanded into the 'Wesleyan Quadrilateral' which adds the fourth category of 'experience' as an additional source of authority. As I've said, we inevitably form our faith in the interaction between our experience and other sources of authority. So here, experience is what I hope you will bring to the conversation, with each of these three dialogue partners in turn.

The first section consists of ways of reading the Bible that are demonstrated or suggested in the Bible itself. Thinking of this as an exercise in nourishment, a book about how to eat healthily and well from the Bible, these ideas are 'from the store cupboard'. That is to say, they are made with ingredients we already have to hand, but which have perhaps ended up at the back of the cupboard unused for years. We often have a rather one-dimensional view of the Bible, and of how it was itself viewed by those who are either depicted in it, or were active participants in writing, transmitting or shaping it. This section uncovers several different ways in which the biblical texts themselves approach and use other biblical texts.

If, for you, the Bible is a trusted friend, you may feel safest here, with familiar names such as King David, Jesus, Saint Paul. Even if you are unsure of the whole premise of this book, having been taught that there is one simple 'plain meaning of Scripture', then I hope you will at least be able to trust the ideas presented in this section, as giving scriptural warrant to or permission for a range of different ways of reading the Bible that must be holy and helpful, since the Bible itself uses them.

Or it may be that these characters from the Bible fall firmly into the category of 'stranger danger' for you. You may have been badly hurt by Bible verses wielded as weapons and feel disinclined to trust their writers as companions on the journey. If so, I hope you might be intrigued by some of the unfamiliar ways even familiar characters in the Bible use Scripture themselves.

The second section introduces ways of reading the Bible from our traditions, from the formational early and medieval history of the Church. I think of this section as 'grandmother's recipe book'. The ideas here are tried and tested and were for centuries the staple diet of the Church. You may recognise some familiar names and notions here, and be interested to see where they come from, and just how ancient they are. Other ideas may seem very alien indeed and extremely strange to modern tastes. As contemporary Christians we tend to have a rather superficial view of what 'the early church' or 'medieval Christians' thought about Scripture; indeed, we often have only a hazy idea of what the differences were between the Church in centuries far wider apart in time from each other than they are from us. We tend to assume and read back a literalism and fundamentalism that the modern period has rejected, when the historical reality is so much more intriguing. Some of these approaches to reading the Bible may be simply historical curiosities but others, even if they appear quaint or unwieldy at first, might be surprisingly helpful to you.

Finally, the third section offers ideas from a range of modern, specialist, even technical approaches to reading the Bible. We might call this section, if we continue the recipe book theme, 'molecular gastronomy'. I love reading contemporary recipe books or watching the sort of cookery programmes that play around with foams, gels and sous vide machines. The fact that I'm never going to attempt those recipes myself in my own kitchen doesn't mean I don't want to hear about them, know what's possible and appreciate more of the artistry and technique behind the finished product when I dine out. In a similar way, we can't all carbon-date an ancient papyrus from our sofas, but if you read a theology book that bases its arguments on such things it is very helpful to have a sense of what is involved. So this is the section that summarises those modern approaches to the Bible that might not be so easy to do at home owing to a lack of technical equipment or technical knowledge, but that you may have heard and wondered about. Form criticism, a hermeneutic of suspicion, performance theory and ecological readings, for example, are covered here, introducing you to some compartments in the toolbox of modern biblical scholarship even if you don't want to go down the road of using them yourself.

How to use this book

I offer this book to you in the hope that it will fundamentally change your approach to reading the Bible. I don't want you to read it purely as an academic or intellectual exercise; I want you to try it out. Experiment. Treat it like a well-loved recipe book, making notes in the margins if you try a substitution that works well for you, or had a culinary disaster. Substitute ingredients or see what happens if you try out a new and experimental combination of two or more of the techniques given here.

Most chapters begin with a sample passage from the Bible, to illustrate or demonstrate the way of Bible reading to be discussed. Then at the end of most chapters, there are some suggestions given for other passages to try reading in this way. These are just examples offered to you as a good place to start, so feel free to apply the method or ideas of that chapter else-where, or to start somewhere different. Please do, though, try the ideas and approaches out; they are of little benefit if you simply read about them and stop there! The nourishment comes in applying them in your own prayerful, playful, exploratory reading of the Bible, and noting what you experience and how you feel about them.

There is no need to read through this book from start to finish. Each chapter is largely self-contained, and where one chapter is linked to another or follows on logically from another it is clearly signposted. So feel free to dip in and out, and to read the sections and chapters in whatever order most takes your interest.

You can read this book either on your own or in a group. If you'd like to use it to form the basis of a Bible study group, Lent course or similar, then I suggest using only a single chapter per session. Some of the chapters include suggestions for group exercises to put what you have read into practice, and more general suggestions for how to run a group study are given at the end of the book in Appendix 2.

PART ONE

From the store cupboard: Scripture

I

Arguing with God

Read: Genesis 18:20–33

Then the LORD said, 'How great is the outcry against Sodom
and Gomorrah and how very grave their sin! I must go
down and see whether they have done altogether according
to the outcry that has come to me; and if not, I will know.'
So the men turned from there, and went towards Sodom,
while Abraham remained standing before the LORD. Then
Abraham came near and said, 'Will you indeed sweep away
the righteous with the wicked? Suppose there are fifty
righteous within the city; will you then sweep away the
place and not forgive it for the fifty righteous who are in it?
Far be it from you to do such a thing, to slay the righteous
with the wicked, so that the righteous fare as the wicked!
Far be that from you! Shall not the Judge of all the earth
do what is just?' And the LORD said, 'If I find at Sodom
fifty righteous in the city, I will forgive the whole place
for their sake.' Abraham answered, 'Let me take it upon
myself to speak to the Lord, I who am but dust and ashes.
Suppose five of the fifty righteous are lacking? Will you
destroy the whole city for lack of five?' And he said, 'I will
not destroy it if I find forty-five there.' Again he spoke to
him, 'Suppose forty are found there.' He answered, 'For
the sake of forty I will not do it.' Then he said, 'Oh do not
let the Lord be angry if I speak. Suppose thirty are found

there.' He answered, 'I will not do it, if I find thirty there.'
He said, 'Let me take it upon myself to speak to the Lord.
Suppose twenty are found there.' He answered, 'For the
sake of twenty I will not destroy it.' Then he said, 'Oh do
not let the Lord be angry if I speak just once more. Suppose
ten are found there.' He answered, 'For the sake of ten I
will not destroy it.' And the LORD went his way, when he
had finished speaking to Abraham; and Abraham returned
to his place.

The book of Genesis is the first, and earliest, part of the
Bible. It contains stories that go back well before the earliest written texts of the Bible were composed, stories that
have been told and retold for thousands of years. For most
of this section, we will be looking at how parts of the Bible
use other, earlier parts of the scriptural tradition – but here
there are no 'earlier' written texts. What we see in the opening chapters of the Bible is the final written form of debates
that went on for hundreds or thousands of years before they
were written down: debates about who God is, what the
world is, and why things are as they are, told in the form of
story and counter-story, and finally combined in the written narrative that we read today. We can see in these early
chapters that, where various different strands of oral tradition didn't combine neatly, they were sometimes kept side
by side – for example, in the two creation stories preserved
in Genesis 1 and 2. And most importantly for our purposes
here, we can see the development of distinctively biblical
ways of thinking about how humans can interact with words
revealed by God.

Words – both God's words, and what they can accomplish,
and how human beings use, misuse and react to words – are
a major theme of the early chapters of Genesis. In Genesis 1,
it is God speaking that calls the world into being. Genesis 2
introduces the idea of God commanding humans not to do

something (in this case, not to eat the fruit from a particular tree). In Genesis 3, for the first time, other characters besides God speak in the narrative – the snake, the woman and the man – and as soon as they take on speaking parts, God's commandment of Genesis 2 is debated and outvoted. Genesis 4 introduces the first argument, resulting in both the first murder and the first lie.

The existence of good and evil is another major theme of these opening chapters. The fundamental assertion of Genesis is that God created the world and created it well. Genesis 1 repeats over and over again the refrain that 'God saw that it was good'. But this begs the question: Then what went wrong? It is observable fact, and always has been, that there is suffering, pain and death in this world. Human beings are capable both of supreme good and appalling evil, and natural disasters or 'acts of God' can seem indiscriminate in who they hurt and what they destroy. The first part of Genesis considers various answers to these age-old questions.

Abraham's negotiation with God in Genesis 18 is the culmination of both of these themes. This story became foundational for the developing biblical understanding of how humans can and should interact with God's word(s) – in dialogue and argument, both directly with a conversation partner, and indirectly with the scriptural tradition so far.

Argument is an important strand in the Jewish rabbinic tradition of reading Scripture. It is what Jesus grew up with. When he stayed behind as a child in the temple (Luke 3:41–9), after a family trip to Jerusalem, and was found 'in the temple courts, sitting among the teachers, listening to them and asking questions', this is the tradition that he was drawn to. He continued with it throughout his adult ministry, debating with 'scribes and pharisees' – though he stayed silent before the outsider, Pilate, who was not trained to appreciate this kind of debate.

It was what rabbis and their disciples did; they wrestled with God, wrestled with the meaning of the Scriptures, in dialogue and debate.

In this rabbinic tradition, still living today, the purpose of argument was and is not so much to arrive at a correct answer as to encounter God in, and let ourselves be formed and changed by, the process of the argument itself. This can be a strange idea to our modern minds. We have mostly been formed by a scientific, post-Enlightenment tradition in which the point of experiments, arguments and debates is to arrive at the truth. We tend to assume that if one reading of the evidence is right, another must be wrong. The quasi-scientific concept of truth that we learn from school is that there is an objective truth to be discovered – even though contemporary science knows things are much more complicated than that.

And so we've tended to approach modern theology and the reading of the Bible in the same way: the point of reading and thinking about it must be to find out the right answers. You may well have heard the Bible referred to as, for example, the 'manufacturer's instruction manual' for human beings. But the Bible isn't organised like an instruction manual, and many of the stories it contains seem to be the opposite of instructions for how to live.

Abraham's negotiation with God in Genesis suggests another way of approaching the Scriptures: as something to be engaged with, wrestled with and argued with. This involves approaching them with reverence, but a very different kind of reverence from what we often mean in the Western cultural tradition. Many of us have been trained from childhood to equate reverence with keeping quiet. A 'reverent silence' was expected in museums, concert halls and churches. We are taught that to show reverence we should look, not touch and listen, not speak. Reverence to a

6

teacher is shown by 'listening respectfully' and not arguing. Even though modern education trends expect more engagement in dialogue, children are still told off in schools for 'arguing back', and authority figures in so many settings — from the Church to politics — react defensively to disagreement. We may find it difficult to think of a robust, experiential approach as 'reverent'.

But the reverence expressed here is the awed expectancy that God might actually listen to us and engage with us in argument - and that both we, and the world, might be permanently changed by the encounter. If you've been brought up in real fear of God's power, the idea of arguing with God might seem terrifying. This story doesn't shy away from that: Abraham is clearly nervous of trying God's patience too far. Another foundational story for the rabbinic tradition is of Jacob wrestling with God in Genesis 32:24–32 — Jacob is left with a permanent limp as a result. Both these stories have a clear message within them that we will survive arguing with God; but also, that we can't expect arguing with God to be a purely academic exercise. Arguing with God, wrestling with the Scriptures, means getting deeply involved. It means taking them, and God, seriously enough to invest time and energy in risking the debate.

These ancient stories also help us to see that many of the biblical texts, which we so often read simply as stand-alone stories, are themselves part of this process of debate. The canon of Scripture preserves these debates for us, so that we can learn not just from the stories themselves and from our reflection on them, but also from reflecting on and debating the relationship between different stories. The fact that the Bible doesn't always agree with itself on everything (unlike that idea of an instruction book) doesn't mean it's not inspired; it means that the process of debate and argument is a (perhaps *the*) place where inspiration happens.

So, for example, one strand of Jewish tradition about the story of Abraham arguing with God over the fate of Sodom and Gomorrah is to understand it as an argument against the idea that natural disasters must be God's will. This stands in dialogue with the story of Noah and the flood (Genesis 6–8), where the whole population of the world is destroyed apart from the eight people in the ark. It is also in dialogue with the story of Adam and Eve, and strands of tradition that interpret all that has gone wrong in the world as God's punishment for their disobedience in eating the apple. Or the story of Cain and Abel in Genesis 4, where jealousy and sibling rivalry is the cause of the first murder. In other words, this whole opening section of Genesis invites us to contemplate various answers to the question of why evil and suffering exist.

In this context, the story of Abraham's lengthy negotiation with God serves to conclude this section with a debate about the morality of punishing the good alongside the wicked. Could God do that? Would God do that? And if not, then natural disasters that destroy whole communities or large swathes of the population should not be blamed on God's anger. It is interesting to compare this story with the book of Jonah, and his mission to tell the wicked inhabitants of the city of Nineveh of God's imminent destruction. Or with the persistence into our own time of the human tendency to claim that illnesses or natural disasters might be God's judgement. 'What have I done to deserve this?' is a perennial human question in the face of suffering. The Bible doesn't give a simple answer. Instead, it tells stories, and invites us to argue with them, to argue even with God, and to find meaning in the very experience of that argument.

So don't hesitate to argue back with God when you read something in the Bible, or encounter a situation in life, that seems to you unjust, unfair or indefensible. What on earth is God doing? Why is this in the Bible at all? How on earth are we meant to make sense of this? Surely God − who's meant to be Love − isn't really like this? These are all perfectly good, healthy and indeed biblical questions to ask. But asking them involves genuinely grappling with God − so don't expect to have your worldview, lifestyle or opinions unchanged as a result.

2

Stories to grab your attention

Read: 2 Samuel 12:1-10

And the LORD sent Nathan to David. He came to him, and said to him, 'There were two men in a certain city, one rich and the other poor. The rich man had very many flocks and herds; but the poor man had nothing but one little ewe lamb, which he had bought. He brought it up, and it grew up with him and with his children; it used to eat of his meagre fare, and drink from his cup, and lie in his bosom, and it was like a daughter to him. Now there came a traveller to the rich man, and he was loath to take one of his own flock or herd to prepare for the wayfarer who had come to him, but he took the poor man's lamb, and prepared that for the guest who had come to him.' Then David's anger was greatly kindled against the man. He said to Nathan, 'As the LORD lives, the man who has done this deserves to die; he shall restore the lamb four-fold, because he did this thing, and because he had no pity.'

Nathan said to David, 'You are the man! Thus says the LORD, the God of Israel: I anointed you king over Israel, and I rescued you from the hand of Saul; I gave you your master's house, and your master's wives into your bosom, and gave you the house of Israel and of Judah; and if that had been too little, I would have added as much more. Why have you despised the word of the LORD, to do what is evil in his sight? You have struck down Uriah the Hittite with the sword, and have taken his wife to be your wife, and have killed him with the sword of the Ammonites. Now therefore the sword shall never depart from your house, for you have despised me, and have taken the wife of Uriah the Hittite to be your wife.

There are several parts of the Bible that make us wince when we read them. Often these are bracketed out in reading plans and lectionaries – few churches will include in their reading of the psalms, for example, the line 'Blessed are those who take your children and dash them against the rocks'. Such blatant examples of religious and racial hatred are often used against Christianity as one reason not to take the Bible seriously. But if we read the whole Bible, and do take it seriously, what are we to make of such passages?

This story from 2 Samuel sees the prophet Nathan challenge King David's appalling behaviour. David has raped or seduced Bathsheba, and then, when she becomes pregnant, he first tries to cover up by getting her husband to come back and sleep with her himself, and when that plan fails, he gives orders for her husband to be killed. In response, God sends the prophet Nathan to challenge David. It is, on the face of it, a rather uninspiring story of privileged male entitlement on the part of someone who is meant to be God's chosen and anointed king, a hero of the tradition.

Nathan's method is not to condemn David outright, but to tell him a story. He tells the story as if he were recounting an actual incident to the king, only later revealing that this is a fictional story that he has composed to make his point. David clearly understands the story to be a factual account of an injustice and reacts as any right-thinking person would be expected to: he is angry at the injustice, greed and misuse of power that the story recounts. And then, because he is the king, that is to say he knows he is in a position of power and is expected to enforce justice when a complaint is brought before him, he demands to know who the wrongdoer is and vows to bring him to account.

This episode, when the prophet Nathan tells David the story and then springs the trap on him, is a key passage when dealing with the parts of the Bible that appal us. Here, the prophet Nathan gives us a model of handling and using story that suggests that what matters about how we respond to these stories is *precisely that we are appalled*.

It does not matter that the story is not, in fact, literally true – that no sheep were harmed in the making of this story. Nathan's purpose in telling the tale is not to get justice for a fictional sheep farmer, but to evoke the reaction that he did in his hearer: to make him angry at the injustice and determined to do something about it. Only then does he point out that it is David's own behaviour that he has just described.

At one level – within the story itself – this is simply a clever way of trapping David into condemning himself. But it is also an example to us of what God might be doing for us, through the inclusion of some really problematic incidents and stories in the canon of Scripture.

There has been a tendency historically to read violent, sexist, racist and otherwise hard texts as if they were both literally *descriptive* of God's will for humanity and *prescriptive* for righteousness. So, for example, passages that tell of genocide as a punishment for unrighteousness have often been read on these two levels. They have been read as if they *describe* incidents that really happened in history and *prescribe* that it is God's will that unrighteousness be destroyed. Such texts have then all too often been used to justify taking destructive action on God's behalf. And, let's be honest, some of them were almost certainly written with exactly that in mind. The biblical texts record the full range of human emotions and desires, including a whole variety of ways in which greed, fear, envy or even the simple desire for security can lead to violence, cruelty and destruction. In many cases it appears that the authors felt they were describing justified, God-given actions, whereas reading their accounts now we recoil from seeing it that way. This is explored further in part 3, particularly in chapters 16-18 exploring aspects of liberation theology.

But Nathan's use of story here suggests an alternative way of reading such episodes, focusing not (for the moment) on the historical and ethical questions they raise, but on the emotions they evoke in us. The parts of the Bible that seem appalling to us might be read as functioning just as Nathan's story did for David. If Nathan had simply described and condemned David's behaviour, then his message would have had much less emotional power. David may well have reacted defensively. He may have attempted to justify himself. He may even have persuaded himself that his own justification was correct, and become more entrenched in his belief that he had a right to act as he did. By telling a story, Nathan first evoked in David something of God's passion for justice and righteousness, so that he was then able to recognise how his own behaviour had violated those ideals.

So when a passage enrages us, this story suggests that the first question to ask is not 'Is it true?' but 'Why am I so angry?' What is it about the behaviour described – whether of people, or of God – that is so appalling to you?

Then consider: how does it change your reading of that passage if you think of its being in the Bible for you now, as you read it today, as being like Nathan telling this story to David. What if the 'teller' of the story suddenly turned round and told you that the reason they'd told this story was to bring you to a fresh realisation of just how appalling such behaviour is? What if 'That's appalling!' is exactly what God wants to say to us through that story being included in the Bible?

And what if you then turn to yourself and hear 'You are the one!' said to you, in response to your righteous anger about the behaviour being described? What happens if you use your revulsion from the passage as a spur to self-examination? If the passage that angers you, that stirs deep feelings of revulsion in you, were being told as a parable, a fictional story-with-a-point to *you*, what point would be being made?

It's not always the case, of course, but very often the things that we recoil most from are things that reveal our own shadows, or our own passions and vocations. Our own shadows because we are often most upset or revolted by behaviour or traits that we subconsciously dislike about ourselves. That isn't to say that we recoil from a passage about murder, for example, because we are literally murderers, but perhaps there is a rigorously suppressed shadow part of your personality that you fear might erupt in violent anger? Perhaps you have a tendency to deny or metaphorically 'kill' any ideas or suggestions that conflict with your own preferences? Or perhaps your strong feelings in response to an upsetting story could reveal something about where your true passions and vocations lie? Is there a call to you to focus your energies on challenging one particular area of the deep injustices of our society?

14

Try reading Genesis 22 or Judges 16 through the lens of
the prophet Nathan's use of story. Keep this perspective in
your Bible reading recipe book and try using it when you next
come across a passage that infuriates you, appals you or even
just irritates you.

3

Meditating on the law

Read: Psalm 1

> Happy are those
> who do not follow the advice of the wicked,
> or take the path that sinners tread,
> or sit in the seat of scoffers;
> but their delight is in the law of the LORD,
> and on his law they meditate day and night.
> They are like trees
> planted by streams of water,
> which yield their fruit in its season,
> and their leaves do not wither.
> In all that they do, they prosper.
> The wicked are not so,
> but are like chaff that the wind drives away.
> Therefore the wicked will not stand in the judgement,
> nor sinners in the congregation of the righteous;
> for the LORD watches over the way of the righteous,
> but the way of the wicked will perish.

Throughout the book of Psalms there is an emphasis on the joy and peace that comes from meditating on 'the law'. It's important to realise that by 'the law' the psalmists don't mean 'rules and regulations', but a much broader and more diffuse category, made up of various concentric circles. At its heart are the ten commandments. Widening our focus, the category of 'law' also includes the context in which those commandments were given – that is, the theological history of Israel contained in the Pentateuch (the first five books of the Bible from Genesis to Deuteronomy). The final circle, wider still, includes all the history and tradition of rabbinical commentary and debate on those books and commandments. It is this whole history and tradition – the contemplation of the action of God in history and story, as well as in specific commandments, and the contemplation of a tradition of argument and debate as well as God's self-revelation – that the psalmists commend to us as nourishing soil to be rooted in and fed by.

This theme is set up in this very first psalm. It reaches its peak in the longest psalm, number 119, which takes the form of an extended acrostic poem (each verse beginning with the next letter of the Hebrew alphabet), where each verse is about the joys, delights and consequences of meditating on the law.

This is a spiritual focus that can seem very alien to modern Christians. We have often been schooled in a simplistic view that Jesus came to replace law with Spirit. After all, Paul's saying that 'the law kills but the Spirit gives life' (2 Corinthians 3:6) is one of the most frequently quoted aphorisms of the epistles. This, coupled with centuries of Christian antisemitism where all law-based religious practices have been demonised as 'pharasaical', can make it hard for us to see any spiritual value in the law.

Yet Jesus, while on occasion radically reinterpreting the law, is also recorded as saying that he had not come to abolish but to fulfil it, and that not the smallest stroke of a letter was obsolete (Matthew 5:17–18). And the psalms, with their emphasis on the beauty of the law as material for meditation, have throughout Christian history been one of the main sources of spiritual reading, both in formal liturgy and in popular devotion. Those beautiful medieval books of hours were largely composed of psalms. Before complete Bibles became widely available the book of Psalms was the most likely book for anyone to own. Singing and chanting the psalms has throughout Christian history been at the core of monastic devotion and remains the core of the residual monastic offices that shape much daily prayer in the Orthodox, Roman Catholic and Anglican traditions.

So what do the psalms mean when they speak of meditating on the law? What can that tell us about how we can use and read Scripture?

The book of Psalms begins with this short song, Psalm 1, which contrasts the 'righteous' person who meditates on the law with the wicked, sinners and mockers. Our modern sensibilities tend to focus immediately on the poor figures of the wicked, and wonder what they have done to deserve such condemnation, so let's begin by reminding ourselves that these are not actual people being described! Rather, these are personifications representing two alternative paths that we might choose to take through life. The song encourages us to take the path of righteousness, and much of the book of Psalms can be read as a commentary on this idea. In the wide variety of songs, poems and thought experiments that make up the book of Psalms, some of the consequences of each of the two paths are fleshed out. The psalmists variously rejoice in being on the path; long to find the right way; panic and cry out in distress when the way seems to have been lost; and anticipate a destination where all creation is united in singing praises to God.

Meditating on the law is, most importantly, described as being natural. Just as a tree drinks water, Psalm 1 implies, we can drink spiritual nourishment from such meditation. It is not presented as a hard task, or something that requires specialist knowledge, skills or equipment. It can be done day and night. And so long as you put yourself in the right place – let your roots go down to the water by choosing to spend time in such meditation – you can confidently expect that the nourishment and fruitfulness that results will come as naturally as tree roots take up water. We're just made that way.

Second, meditating on the law is described as both a desire and a delight. This is very far from our usual contemporary view of law. We might think of law at its most positive as something that is necessary to guard against disorder, but it's hard to imagine it as a source of joy and delight in its own right! Similarly, we tend to think nowadays of religious rules, commandments or prohibitions, as at best some sort of grim religious duty that we won't enjoy but might, we suppose, be good for us – like fibre in our diet perhaps. However, this is clearly not the kind of law that the psalmists have in mind. In the psalms, spending time meditating on God's law is consistently described as something that we long for, thirst for, and that brings us joy. The theme of thirsting and longing recurs throughout the book of Psalms, most famously in the opening lines of Psalm 42: 'As the deer pants for streams of water, so my soul pants for you, my God. My soul thirsts for God'. This is the language of desire, and it resonates with the extraordinary way in which sexual longing and physical desire are described in the Song of Songs, variously interpreted as a literal love poem and/or an extended allegory of our desire for God, and quite possibly deliberately intending to draw out the parallels between the two. As Augustine of Hippo put it, in describing how all our natural human desires point to our desire for God, 'You have made us for yourself, and our hearts are restless until they find their rest in you' (*Confessions* 1.1.1).

The image of the branching roots of a tree reaching deep into the soil for nourishment can help us separate out some of the strands of what the psalms mean by this meditation, and how it can help us read the Bible, and read it joyfully rather than simply dutifully.

Think of the soil first. Psalm 1 imagines 'the law' – the whole tradition of those concentric circles of commandments,

Pentateuch, and reflection and thought about them – as the soil that our roots can be firmly anchored in. Rootedness in tradition is important, Psalm 1 argues. It will keep us standing firm when adverse weather comes in our lives and our faith. The firmly rooted tree is contrasted with chaff – the dry, dead husks that are discarded when wheat is threshed – blown about wherever the wind takes it. A similar image that recurs elsewhere in the psalms is that of 'dwelling' in the house of God. Psalm 52 even combines both of these images into one: 'I am like an olive tree flourishing in the house of God'. A recurring theme of the psalms is that good and bad times will come to everyone, and so it is important to have stability and resilience built into our faith. Being rooted in the tradition of contemplating the Scriptures is a key way of doing that.

But roots aren't just about stability and fixedness. Roots are growing, living things, and are always themselves on a journey, seeking out and growing towards water and nourishment. Longing, desire, seeking, inquiring, being led to and following the right path are all also important and recurring themes in the psalms' contemplation of what it is to meditate on the law.

There is learning and teaching involved. But it is not the kind of functional teaching that is about imparting and obtaining knowledge. The learning and teaching that the writer of Psalm 119 describes as making them wiser than either teachers or the aged isn't primarily about obtaining knowledge but about developing understanding. The psalms stand in the Wisdom tradition of the Bible, which has its equivalents in most worldwide spiritual traditions, where understanding – 'enlightenment', perhaps, is the contemporary equivalent term – comes from spending time in contemplation of paradoxes, mysteries and seemingly simple things.

So try reading the Bible not as a textbook to be learned and applied, but as soil to be rooted in and fed by. Try this especially with those first five books of the Bible – Genesis, for example, or Exodus. When you read a passage, imagine that you are putting your roots down into it. Roots that aren't fixed, wooden things but living, seeking tendrils, probing thirstily through the earth, seeking what nourishment may be found there.

It may help to write out or print out a passage that you are focusing on, and then draw a simple diagram of a tree growing out of it. Try this, for example, with Genesis 3, or Genesis 18:1–15, or Deuteronomy 5:1–22. Sketch a trunk, and then sketch roots going down into the words of the text. Which words or phrases are they seeking out to draw nourishment from? If they go off the side of the page, what else are they looking for? If they go down below the words themselves to the empty space at the bottom of the page, what's the living water that they are seeking beneath the ground of these words?

And then sketch branches, leaves and fruit growing from the tree trunk that is rooted in this passage. What branches of thought come from this ground? What fruit does it produce in you?

4

Fulfilment

Read: Luke 4:16–21

> When he came to Nazareth, where he had been brought up, he went to the synagogue on the sabbath day, as was his custom. He stood up to read, and the scroll of the prophet Isaiah was given to him. He unrolled the scroll and found the place where it was written:
>
> > 'The Spirit of the Lord is upon me,
> > because he has anointed me
> > to bring good news to the poor.
> > He has sent me to proclaim release to the captives
> > and recovery of sight to the blind,
> > to let the oppressed go free,
> > to proclaim the year of the Lord's favour.'
>
> And he rolled up the scroll, gave it back to the attendant, and sat down. The eyes of all in the synagogue were fixed on him. Then he began to say to them, 'Today this scripture has been fulfilled in your hearing.'

Fulfilment is a major theme in the way that both Jesus himself, and the four Gospel writers, quote the Hebrew Scriptures. Jesus describes himself on several occasions as fulfilling Scripture, either in his very presence or in particular actions. And all sorts of details in the events described in the Gospels are attributed by the Gospel writers or editors as having happened in order to fulfil prophecies.

Reading the Old Testament in the light of Christ is clearly inevitable for Christians. We all read everything in the light of our accumulated knowledge and experience. But we need to be wary: there is a long history of Christians reading the Old Testament through the lens of Christ's claims to fulfilment in an antisemitic way, arguing that the covenant with the people of Israel was lacking and provisional. Another objection to simplistic christological readings of the Old Testament comes from modern historical scholarship, pointing out that when such readings are taken as the only or 'true' meaning of a passage, they obscure the meaning and interpretation of the original text as a historical artefact — or as inspired Scripture — in its own right and on its own terms. So the questions for us to grapple with, as we seek to read the Bible in a way that is both scripturally faithful and nourishing for our faith, are: What did Jesus and the Gospel writers mean by 'fulfilment'? And how can we avoid the problems that this type of reading has sometimes had?

The word 'fulfil' has a broad collection of meanings. In both the original Greek and in our English translation, 'fulfil' can have not only a literal transactional overtone (as when an online supplier 'fulfils' your order) but also a more figurative implication of plenitude and abundance. The same word is used when we read of valleys being 'filled in' and mountains and hills made low (Luke 3:5); Jesus being 'filled' with wisdom as he grew up (Luke 2:40); a house being 'filled' with the smell of perfume (John 12:3); and a house being 'filled' with the sound of rushing wind at Pentecost (Acts 2:2).

The Gospels use both these meanings of 'fulfilment' in different places, and much of the difficulty can be avoided if they are not confused. First, and most simply, in some places the Gospels clearly use the idea of Jesus fulfilling prophecy in a way that implies a completed transaction. A particular action or wording is described as having fulfilled a prophecy made in the past. That prophecy is in effect 'ticked off' a cosmic list of as-yet-unfulfilled prophecies. Such claims were common in the ancient world. They formed a recognised genre of argument and evidence, with similar claims being made about Roman emperors, for example, fulfilling prophecy.

For all four Gospel writers, one of the main reasons that this idea of Jesus fulfilling prophecy was important lay in answering the question of how on earth God could have allowed God-self incarnate – God's dearly beloved Son, the anointed one – to die. This was such a radical and blasphemous idea that it needed a lot of justification. The idea that, in dying, Jesus was fulfilling scriptural prophecy seems to have been the preferred answer of the early church. Many of the Gospel references to fulfilment occur in the crucifixion narratives themselves, or the lead up to the crucifixion, echoing this sense of a climactic moment, a culmination. In John's Gospel, of course, Jesus' last words from the cross are 'It is finished', which might just as easily be translated 'It is completed' or 'It has been fulfilled' (John 19:30). Notice that while this is the completion of Jesus' human life on earth, of his vocational task if you like, and certainly a (or even the) climactic moment in the Bible, it is not the end of the story. The story of God's relationship with the world and with humanity continues: in the resurrection appearances, in the commissioning and development of the early church, and in us today and all who live beyond the last page of the Bible.

Second, the Gospels use the idea of fulfilment in the sense of making something more full – filling it up, fleshing it out. Jesus' incarnation is portrayed in the Gospel accounts as very literally 'fleshing out' the framework of what we know about God from the law and the prophets (the Latin word 'carne', from which 'incarnation' is derived, literally means 'meat' or

24

'flesh'). Jesus, for Christians, is God made human; simultaneously fully human, and fully divine. Jesus is God's self-revelation, and God is as God is in Jesus. We hold that together with our belief that God is also revealed through Scripture, and through the history of how God has related with the world that Scripture records, reflects on, and shows some very human struggles with.

Again, for all four Gospel writers, references to Jesus fulfilling the Scriptures cluster around both the beginning and end of the story, around Jesus' birth and death. Fulfilment as a concept and theme frames the way in which the story of Jesus is presented to us. This use of fulfilment to frame the story of Jesus is especially explicit in Luke's Gospel, which begins with Luke's prologue describing why he has written and arranged the material that he puts before us. Here (1:1), Luke refers to the Gospel as 'an account of the things that have been fulfilled among us'. And as we read in the extract with which this chapter began, Jesus begins his public ministry by announcing himself as the fulfilment of this passage of Isaiah. Thus begins his struggle with those who consider this to be a blasphemous claim.

One of the most memorable aspects of Luke's account of the resurrection is the climactic encounter on the road to Emmaus (Luke 24:13–35), where this theme of Jesus fulfilling 'the law of Moses, the prophets and the psalms' is emphasised in Jesus' long teaching session with the disciples as they travel. Understanding this, their eyes are opened and they are able to see Jesus in the breaking of the bread. For Luke, this is part of the astonishing truth about who Jesus is: in Jesus, in this man in front of you, the Scriptures are being fulfilled. It's the beginning and end of the story.

The mistake that centuries of antisemitic readings of this idea of fulfilment have made is to confuse these two meanings. The idea of completion has too often been read as a negation of all that has gone before, as if the law and the prophets have now been ticked off, finished and no longer have any relevance. But this way of thinking is one that Jesus' words in Matthew 5:17 specifically warn us against: 'Do not think that I have come to abolish the Law or the Prophets; I have not come to abolish them but to fulfil them' (NIV). This is not 'fulfilment' in the sense that your online shopping order has been fulfilled and is now done and dusted. Rather, it is 'fulfilment' in the sense that you find fulfilment in your work, your family, your friends — they make life whole and wholesome, full of meaning and joy. This fulfilment is an ongoing state, not a one-off transaction.

How, then, does this affect how we read the Old Testament as Christians? First, it is important to remember that Scripture is too rich to have only a single meaning. We'll come to this idea in more detail in the second part of this book, where we'll look at how medieval interpreters separated out four potential layers of meaning, but for now try to read the Scriptures with a double awareness. First, let yourself be aware of what the text might have meant, or how it might have been heard, in its original context. Second, let yourself be aware of what resonances it has for you in the light of the story of Jesus. It's not the case that one of these is the correct reading, and one is wrong. Nor is it the case that the text 'needs' the additional layer of meaning that we might see in it as Christians; remember, Jesus told the lawyer who asked him what he needed for salvation, that what he read in the law was sufficient (Luke 10:21–31). But we can't help but see resonances and patterns as we read the Hebrew Scriptures as Christians.

As you read in this way, bear in mind the two distinct interpretative 'keys' of the incarnation and the cross. These correspond to the two different shades of meaning of the word 'fulfilment': fleshing out and completion.

So when you read an Old Testament passage, try asking yourself the following questions. You could try this, for example, with Exodus 14 or 16, with 1 Samuel 3 or Ezekiel 2.

- Are there any words, phrases or images in this passage that strike a chord with words, phrases or images from the Gospels? If so, what are the similarities and differences? Notice that these resonances are there in your mind, fleshing out your reading almost without your conscious involvement.
- Is there anything in the setting or narrative of this passage that the Gospel writers might have been consciously or unconsciously echoing as they arranged their material into the Gospels we have today?
- How does what you know of Jesus flesh out what God might be communicating to you in your reading of this passage?
- Is there anything started, or unfinished, in this passage or the wider narrative context that seems to be rounded off or completed in some way in Jesus/the Gospel narratives?
- Does this story leave you with the sense that there are still loose ends, unfinished business, remaining today – whether in your life, in the life of the Church, or in the world?

Introduction to chapters 5 and 6: the use and misuse of Scripture in Jesus' temptations

Read: Matthew 4:1–11

Then Jesus was led up by the Spirit into the wilderness to be tempted by the devil. He fasted for forty days and forty nights, and afterwards he was famished. The tempter came and said to him, 'If you are the Son of God, command these stones to become loaves of bread.' But he answered, 'It is written,

> "One does not live by bread alone,
> but by every word that comes from the mouth of God."'

Then the devil took him to the holy city and placed him on the pinnacle of the temple, saying to him, 'If you are the Son of God, throw yourself down; for it is written,

> "He will command his angels concerning you",
> and "On their hands they will bear you up,
> so that you will not dash your foot against a stone."'

Jesus said to him, 'Again it is written, "Do not put the Lord your God to the test."'
   Again, the devil took him to a very high mountain and showed him all the kingdoms of the world and their splendour; and he said to him, 'All these I will give you, if you will

fall down and worship me.' Jesus said to him, 'Away with you, Satan! for it is written,

> "Worship the Lord your God,
> and serve only him.'"

Then the devil left him, and suddenly angels came and waited on him.

This passage is read in many Christian churches at the beginning of Lent. Most commonly, when we reflect on this passage in Lent, we are thinking about the nature of temptation and the things that tempt us – money, material objects, things that satisfy our appetites, power, glory, fame, and so on. But in this pair of chapters, I want us to think about this passage as something of a miniature masterclass in the use and misuse of Scripture.

What we have depicted here is a dialogue, a conversation, in which scriptural references are thrown around like ammunition. This is what a lot of people think theological discussion is like and live in fear of! Many people have told me that the main reason they avoid talking to other people about their faith is precisely that they fear this kind of conversation being the result, because they don't feel that they know their Bible well enough not to let God down in such an exchange.

However, I think we can be pretty sure that this is not given to us as a model of ideal theological discussion, if only from the fact that Jesus' conversation partner here is not another person but 'the devil', 'the tempter', 'Satan'. This is a set of shadowy and elusive terms for a character that modern culture tends to think of in rather pantomime terms. Interestingly, however, this was not a character that was an established part of Jewish faith in Jesus' time. There was no cultural frame of reference at the time that was the equivalent of the red-faced, black-horned, pitchfork-wielding demons of our modern cultural imagination. What the Gospels seem to be describing here are the embodiment of the strong but shadowy forces of temptation that we all experience – the voices that whisper in our head that we deserve this, could do that, could get away with it ...

But for now, let's take the references to 'the devil' at face value and accept that we are reading this as the script of a drama, with Jesus and his antagonist as the two characters depicted in the scene. We are eavesdropping on a conversation that speaks to us about how we might use the Bible, for good or for ill, and invites us to reflect on our own use of Scripture.

In the following two chapters, we will explore two aspects of this dialogue. First, in chapter 5, we will look at the implications of the particular quotations that Jesus uses, and consider how following back quotations to their source is like following a waymarked trail of clues back through the pages of the Bible, to find a fuller understanding of the text. Then in chapter 6, we will focus on how the tempter in this passage uses Scripture, and what that might teach us about the use and misuse of Biblical quotations.

5

Following a waymarked trail

If we think of the Bible as a forest, it is a dense one. The path that others have trod can be faint, and the waymarks that previous travellers have used to blaze the trail for us can be quite hard to spot. It can be difficult to tell whether something is a clue to the trail that the author intended or just an incidental detail – or a later addition. But sometimes the writers try to make it clearer for us by deliberately quoting earlier parts of Scripture. When a passage is as dense with such references as this account of Jesus' temptation in the book of Matthew, it is hard to miss, but quotations are not always so clearly marked or so densely clustered.

In most Bibles, you'll see footnotes when a passage quotes an earlier piece of Scripture, giving you the reference to where you can find the original. These may look like they are only for specialists, but it is often well worth looking them up. When a biblical writer quotes another, earlier, biblical book, they would usually have known the context of what they were quoting. They weren't often just quoting a phrase or sentence as a clincher to an argument. Rather, when a quotation is given it acts as a shorthand for the whole story or debate from the past that is being referenced. When biblical characters or writers quote Scripture, they would normally have expected their first listeners not only to have heard the actual words that they quoted, but also to have been aware of the context and the story that they came from, and understood all that was being alluded to in shorthand form. So it is well worth following up these quotations, and immersing ourselves in the full implications and flavour of what is being said. Reading the Bible while tracing back this trail feels a bit like being a detective, following clues which take you deeper and deeper into the meaning of the text.

Let's look at the specific quotations that both Jesus and the tempter use in this passage. Jesus' quotations all come from the book of Deuteronomy (Deuteronomy 8:3, 6:16 and 6:13), while the tempter quotes Psalm 91:11–12. Deuteronomy is the last of the first five books of the Bible, the Pentateuch. It ends with the death of Moses, concluding the narrative of the Exodus. Deuteronomy is also the first book in the series of histories, making it a pivot for the self-understanding of Israel. It has a particular focus on the land of Israel, on the covenant relationship between God and Israel the people, and on the link between those two things.

Jesus' quotations all come from chapters 6 to 8, a section immediately following the giving of the ten commandments to Moses, and focusing on how important it is for Israel to keep those commandments. In the quotes used here we see the whole story of Israel's wilderness experience summarised. The temptations that Jesus experiences at the end of his forty days in the desert are presented as mirroring the temptations that Israel experienced in their symbolic forty years in the desert: tempted by hunger, tempted to put God to the test, tempted to idolatry. These words are not simply to be taken at face value as clinching arguments or statements of faith; they are deliberately chosen to evoke the story of Israel's wilderness experience and to imply that Jesus is personifying the story of Israel.

The mention of a desire for bread in the desert would have instantly made any of the original Jewish hearers think of the story of manna in the wilderness (Exodus 16). Jesus' reply deliberately references this. Here are the verses from Deuteronomy 8 that his quotation is drawn from:

> Remember the long way that the LORD your God has led you these forty years in the wilderness, in order to humble you, testing you to know what was in your heart, whether or not you would keep his commandments. He humbled you by letting you hunger, then by feeding you with manna, with which neither you nor your ancestors were acquainted, in order to make you understand that one does not live by bread alone, but by every word that comes from the mouth of the LORD. (vv. 2–3)

Immediately, the link between Jesus' forty days in the desert and the Israelite's wilderness experience is made explicit. This continues in Jesus' second quotation. 'Do not put the Lord your God to the test,' he says. The full quotation from Deuteronomy 6:16 reads 'Do not put the LORD your God to the test as you did at Massah' (NIV) Early Jewish hearers of the Gospel would probably have completed that quotation in their heads, and known to what Massah referred. We who are less immersed in the Hebrew Scriptures probably need a quick online search to discover that Massah is a reference to Exodus 17. In that passage, having been miraculously fed with manna and quail, the people of Israel continue to journey, but they now experience an even more serious danger – a lack of water to drink. Here's the incident:

The people quarrelled with Moses, and said, 'Give us water to drink' ... So Moses cried out to the Lord, 'What shall I do with this people? They are almost ready to stone me.' The Lord said to Moses, 'Go on ahead of the people, and take some of the elders of Israel with you; take in your hand the staff with which you struck the Nile, and go ... Strike the rock, and water will come out of it, so that the people may drink.' Moses did so, in the sight of the elders of Israel. He called the place Massah and Meribah, because the Israelites quarrelled and tested the Lord, saying, 'Is the Lord among us or not?'(Exodus 17:2, 4–7)

That final demand, 'Is the Lord among us or not?' points to the central question about Jesus that the Gospels are written to answer.

Lastly, Jesus quotes Deuteronomy 6:13, 'Worship the Lord your God, and serve only him'. Having been reminded of the story of the Israelites' desert experience it would not have been hard for the first hearers of Matthew's Gospel to make the connection both with the stories of the Israelites creating and worshipping a golden calf while Moses was away on the mountain receiving the ten commandments, and also with all the dire warnings in Deuteronomy not to follow the gods of other societies or cultures.

This final temptation suddenly expands the frame of reference from simply a reminder of the history and founding myths of Israel, to the reality that these words are being spoken and heard in a multicultural society under occupation. The vision of ruling over all, as far as the eye could see from the highest point of the temple, evokes the claims of the Roman Empire to domination and rule over all the known world. This is starkly contrasted with the claims and promises of God to the people of Israel. The listener is therefore presented with a choice: faithfulness to the covenant or allying yourself to

Rome's claims to glory, and the Roman emperor's claim to divinity.

In just a few lines, then, this passage demonstrates how the biblical writers used nested quotations and imagery. By making simple references to what would have been well-known stories, they are able to say much more than the brevity of each text might suggest on first reading. Following back the footnotes helps us to understand the full context of each quotation and the range of imagery, history and shared cultural understanding that each one could have evoked in the first hearers of the Gospels.

This is all part of the plain meaning of the text, and without it our understanding is impoverished. If we read this story simply as a battle of wits between Jesus and a demon – or if we dismiss it because we can't take the idea of a talking demon seriously – we could easily overlook some of its layers of meaning. We could easily miss that this passage is not *only* about temptation (as it undoubtedly is) but *also* about positioning Jesus as recapitulating in his own person the salvation history of Israel.

When you are reading the Bible and see several other Scripture passages quoted, it is very often worth looking them up and seeing whether there is more to the story than merely the words being used. A simple clue that there might be a trail to follow is when you see a long list of Scripture references in the footnotes at the bottom of the page. Don't just look up the single verse that is quoted: take the time to read the whole section that is being referred to. You might even want to look that passage up in a commentary to find out more about it.

Then consider what questions are being asked in the original passage that this quotation is answering or addressing. How does the wider context of the quotation feed into answering those questions? Does it make things simpler or does it open our eyes to deeper complexity? What light does this quotation in its original context shine on the nature of God or the nature of faith? What difference does it make if you imagine that the author or teller of the story assumed that their hearers would know what the quotations are alluding to?

6

The devil quotes Scripture

The second thing to note from the story of Jesus' temptations is that Scripture can be used both for good and for ill. It is perfectly possible to pick out accurate quotations from the Bible and utilise them for unhealthy and destructive purposes, as the character of the tempter does here. This passage demonstrates both the use and the misuse of Scripture and gives us some important principles to exercise in telling them apart.

The temptations begin simply, with a basic appeal to two fundamental human needs: hunger and a sense of identity. The temptation is not simply to satisfy the very real hunger that Jesus would have felt after his fast, but also to satisfy the equally fundamental desire that we have as human beings to know who we are, and to have our identity and our value affirmed. In fact, this question of identity, rather than simple hunger, is the main point of this temptation. Jesus has completed his fast in the desert at this point. There would be nothing at all wrong with him eating bread. The point of the temptation is not that bread would be nice but should be resisted; it's in that weaselly 'if' at the beginning of the sentence: '*If you are* the Son of God ...'

That 'if' calls Jesus' sense of identity into question. It challenges him to test out the affirmation that he received at his baptism immediately prior to his time of fasting and prayer. This doubt-demon can destroy relationships - our relationship with God, and indeed human relationships. It's the same voice that whispers inside our heads 'Do you really love me? Can you prove it to me, again? Will that assurance hold up if I check your phone?' Nothing will ever be enough to satisfy this line of questioning. Assurances given will always be questioned, assurances repeated will be dismissed with 'Well you would say that, wouldn't you?' Our hunger for love and for the assurance of love is bottomless.

In response to this whisper of self-doubt, Jesus reaches for a quote from Deuteronomy. As we saw in the previous section, although superficially the question and answer are both about bread, the deeper meaning of the quotation references the whole hinterland of Israel's wilderness experience. In doing so, it answers not only the question about bread, but also this question about identity. In reaching for a quotation from the Pentateuch, Jesus finds a firm place to stand in the tradition, history and religious experience of his culture and context. It's as if he is saying, '*If* I'm the Son of God? Well, I'm certainly a Son of Israel. *This* is my heritage, *these* are the promises I can claim and *this* is the greater story in which my own story takes on a wider meaning. My identity as a beloved child of God is unshakeable, because it rests on these firm foundations'.

Jesus uses Scripture here as a firm foundation stone, a place to stand. We might be reminded of the parable of the wise and foolish builders who built their houses on rock and sand (Matthew 7:24–7). Both looked like suitable houses, both had as much care taken in their construction, but when storms came only one was able to endure because of its firm foundations. It's not incidental that the quotation Jesus reaches for here comes from the Pentateuch, those first five books of the Bible that were foundational for Jewish faith and self-understanding. Knowing your roots is important for being able to stand firm when your sense of identity is questioned. This in itself provides a good reason to read the Bible and be familiar with its core stories. When all is going well, you may not feel you need it; but when things are difficult, having that foundation to stand firm on can be a lifeline.

Here Jesus has managed to reaffirm his sense of identity with an appeal to a foundational story in the history of Israel. But then his confidence in Scripture is itself questioned. It might be true that the Bible says that; but what about the fact that it also says this?

What I particularly want you to notice about the devil's use of Scripture here is that what is quoted is both *accurate* and *true*. It's quite common to hear it said that the devil lies, or the devil twists Scripture for his uses. But that's not what's going on here. The psalm quoted (Psalm 91) is a beautiful poem about the assurance of God's protection, and it is accurately quoted. It's not that the tempter has taken a quotation out of context or twisted it to mean the opposite of what it really says. The point is that we can tie ourselves up in knots so easily if we allow ourselves to be drawn into the game of playing one piece of the Bible off against another. Which has priority? If the texts contradict each other, which is right? Effectively, the temptation is for Jesus to say 'The Bible says it, so I believe it' and to be drawn into dramatic, self-destructive action to prove — to himself or to others — that he really does believe it. And again, Jesus refers back to the Exodus narrative, part of the theological bedrock of his faith. Believing this, his identity is secure, and he has no need to demonstrate it, to himself or to anyone else who might be watching.

How often have you heard, when people are quoting the Bible, something like 'If you are really a Christian ...' or 'If you really believed that the Bible is the Word of God ...'? Or it might be that it's your own internal monologue that attacks you like this. What can we learn from how Jesus handles his conversation with the tempter, about how to handle these unhelpful voices and unhealthy uses of Scripture?

First, don't waste time arguing about the accuracy or truth of a scriptural reference. Sometimes these will be taken out of context or be based on mistranslations, but often they are completely accurate. It is true that Psalm 91 says what the devil quotes in our passage. It's true that parts of the Bible say that women should behave in certain ways, or that only certain relationships are acceptable, or that people with less than bodily perfection can't serve God liturgically, or that violence is an acceptable answer to certain questions. What Jesus models here is: 'Yes, that's true, the Bible does say that, but this other perspective is also true, and this is more foundational for my faith'. Remember that, when someone asks you what Jesus would do or say, replying 'That's true, but so is this, and for me this is foundational' is a valid way to read the Bible. It is one that Jesus explicitly sanctions and models for us here.

Second, use your common sense. The vital question in our text is not whether this is truly something that the Bible says but whether Jesus should take a very specific dangerous action based on it. It's remarkably liberating to realise that even Jesus doesn't believe that you should always act on what the Bible literally says! Just because Psalm 91 says 'he will command his angels' to protect you, doesn't mean you should jump off a high building. What is healthy and life-giving in a given situation is a sensible – and, from this example, biblical – question to ask. What would Jesus do? Sometimes he'd tell the tempter to stop being stupid.

Third, be alert to any sentence that runs 'If ... then ...'! Don't act out of a desire to prove your love, or your faith, to anyone watching. Your relationship with God is more important than what anyone else thinks of it, or of you – you don't need to prove it to anyone. And conversely, don't act out of a desire to get God to prove to you that you are loved. Comparison is the enemy of joy. Resist the temptation to say to God, 'If you loved me as much as you loved her, then ...' or 'If you're really there and care about me, then ...'

And finally, know where you stand. Spend time reading, reflecting on and praying through the foundations of your faith – before you need it. Jesus has just spent a long silent retreat in the wilderness at this point. This hasn't made him more vulnerable to temptation. On the contrary, it has made him better able to withstand it because he is immersed in his faith and sure of his roots. Spend time reading the Bible. Go on retreats. Pray. Be part of a church community. So that when the demons of self-doubt come whispering – as I can almost guarantee they will – you have the bedrock of your inheritance of faith on which to stand firm.

7

A great cloud of witnesses

Read: Hebrews 11:1–12.2 (abridged here):

Now faith is the assurance of things hoped for, the conviction of things not seen. Indeed, by faith our ancestors received approval ... By faith Noah, warned by God about events as yet unseen, respected the warning and built an ark to save his household ... By faith Abraham obeyed when he was called to set out for a place that he was to receive as an inheritance; and he set out, not knowing where he was going ... By faith he received power of procreation, even though he was too old – and Sarah herself was barren ... By faith Moses was hidden by his parents for three months after his birth ... By faith the walls of Jericho fell [and] by faith Rahab the prostitute did not perish ... And what more should I say? For time would fail me to tell [of all who] administered justice, obtained promises, shut the mouths of lions, quenched raging fire, escaped the edge of the sword, won strength out of weakness, became mighty in war, put foreign armies to flight ... suffered mocking and flogging, and even chains and imprisonment ... Therefore, since we are surrounded by so great a cloud of witnesses, let us also lay aside every weight and the sin that clings so closely, and let us run with perseverance the race that is set before us, looking to Jesus the pioneer and perfecter of our faith.

How do we know what we know, not just about God, but about anything? A typical modern answer is that we learn through our own experience, through a scientific process of experimentation and deduction. But dig a little bit deeper and it becomes clear that we take most things on trust. We know things that we have been taught, or that we have read, because we trust the witness of those who have passed them on to us. This is as true in modern science and academia as it is in daily life and in faith.

As we become more aware of the ease with which misinformation and propaganda can spread through social media, schools are increasingly teaching children how to review their sources of information. We're becoming uneasily aware of the possibility of 'deep fakes', and of the danger of spreading plausible-sounding stories by a simple 'like' on our social media feed. The unreliability of information may seem like a uniquely modern question, but propaganda − trying to control the story − has always been a tool of the powerful, the manipulative, and the con artist, whatever technology they have had at their disposal. The early Christians were working out their faith in a bewildering multifaith context, where those claiming to be magicians, prophets and miracle-workers were a common sight in every market place. How were they to know which of the travelling preachers who claimed to be Christians, or which of the letters which claimed to be from Paul, were to be taken seriously? How were they to tell who was bringing authentic teaching, and who was a false prophet or simply a snake-oil salesman out for their own gain?

In the reading above, the writer of Hebrews draws attention, in the midst of competing arguments and claims about the shape and direction that the early churches should take, to the foundational importance of the witness of the Old Testament, the Hebrew Scriptures. As we saw in the previous chapter when looking at Jesus' temptation in the desert, the idea of being steeped in the stories of the Scriptures gives us a firm foundation, in a world where everything might not be what it seems. Having a firm place to stand, we can then trust ourselves to look out at the myriad competing options and truth claims that are held out before us and trust ourselves to make sensible decisions about them. Hebrews suggests that we view the Bible as a collection of witness statements. They are evidence, handed down to us over time, of the interaction of God with God's people and/or God's world.

Witness statements often conflict with one another over details. They describe the same or different facets of an event from widely different perspectives. Sometimes what they say is true, sometimes it's an outright lie told for propaganda purposes; often it's a combination of what the witness thinks is true and their own cultural blindspots or assumptions. Witness statements are written for a purpose. Sometimes that purpose is obvious, sometimes it is more complex — and part of the task of assessing witness statements is to ask why they are telling us what they do.

Combine this idea of witness statements with Paul's image of us running a relay race through time in which the baton is now handed on to us. This suggests that we take a multi-tiered historical approach to reading the Bible. First, there is the actual historical experience that led to any one passage of Scripture being written in the first place — the creation of the baton. Second, there's the fact that this particular story was chosen as one that was transmitted down through time, whether verbally or in writing, over the generations. Third, there's its effect on us as we read it now, and the question of what we do as a result; and finally, there's our part in passing it on to future generations.

In the first place, reading the Bible as witness statements means taking what is included seriously as a record of some sort of experience. This does not, of course, mean assuming that everything literally happened. To take an obvious example, many of the best-known stories in the prophets, such as Ezekiel's vision of the valley of the dry bones (Ezekiel 37:1–14), do not for a moment claim to be describing actual historical incidents, but they do claim to be describing an actual prayer experience that the prophet had. Many of us will have similar 'visions' or imaginative experiences of God showing us something in a time of prayer or in a dream (see chapter 14). It is not always so clear from the text whether or not what is being described claims to be an actual historical incident, but bear in mind as you read that *something* has happened that has caused the original author to write or tell this story.

Second, be aware of the historical fact that the passage you are reading is one that generations of people have chosen to tell, retell, write down and pass on to those who came after them. It's obvious that the Bible doesn't describe everything that has ever happened! Ask yourself why, of all the incidents and writings and oral traditions that could have been chosen to pass on to us, this particular text became one of the selected few. (We'll look at the darker side of this in chapter 17, on the hermeneutics of suspicion). What might past generations have found in this passage that made it an important one for them to collect and pass on? If it's a text that you have tended to read very much in the light of the New Testament (for example, it can be virtually impossible for those of us raised as Christians to read some of the messianic prophecies in Isaiah without hearing them in the context of a Christmas service) then it's worth asking why people before Jesus found this so profound. Are there relatively timeless truths that these stories present, or might they

45

have been heard very differently in some of the various time periods and political contexts through which they've been passed down?

Third, we come to the present day. It is a historical reality that this passage has been passed on to you, as you sit and read it now. Whatever it meant to people in the past, it is now for you, in this moment. Ask yourself what is there about this passage that might make it for you one of the 'great cloud of witnesses' that the writer of Hebrews describes? Is there anything about it that might give you one of the benefits Hebrews describes – something that might help you to disentangle yourself, or free yourself, from something that threatens to hold you back? Something that might give you strength to persevere? Something that directs your focus to Jesus?

And fourth, remember that the Christian faith doesn't begin and end with us. We are running, as it were, one lap of a race; others have been before, and others will come after us. The great cloud of witnesses in Scripture includes the roll call of great heroes and heroines that the writer names, but also countless anonymous others who simply lived their lives – happily or unhappily, peacefully or under situations of great pain and difficulty – and in doing so became part of the inheritance of faith that we receive and pass on. Some had particularly dramatic or spiritual jobs to do, others are commended for more routine activities such as administering justice or (like Moses' mother) for quiet resistance. This idea of us as simply a lap in the relay is both daunting, in its call to us to pass on what we have read and learned to those who come after us, and liberating, in its reminder that God's salvation of the world does not depend on us getting everything right.

Try taking a piece of paper and dividing it into four quarters. Label them 'First', 'Then', 'Now' and 'Next'. Then, as you read a passage of Scripture, make notes in each of the four quadrants, in whatever order you wish, making sure that you consider each of these four historical 'laps'. If you are doing this in a group, you could put up four flipchart pages with these labels, ask people to write down their insights on sticky notes and add them to the relevant sheet. If you find that one quarter is much emptier than the rest, spend additional time, either alone or in a group, thinking about what you might put there.

PART TWO

Grandmother's recipe book: tradition

8

Lectio divina: 'The Ladder of Monks'

Read: John 4:7–15

A Samaritan woman came to draw water, and Jesus said to her, 'Give me a drink'. (His disciples had gone to the city to buy food.) The Samaritan woman said to him, 'How is it that you, a Jew, ask a drink of me, a woman of Samaria?' (Jews do not share things in common with Samaritans.) Jesus answered her, 'If you knew the gift of God, and who it is that is saying to you, "Give me a drink", you would have asked him, and he would have given you living water.' The woman said to him, 'Sir, you have no bucket, and the well is deep. Where do you get that living water? Are you greater than our ancestor Jacob, who gave us the well, and with his sons and his flocks drank from it?' Jesus said to her, 'Everyone who drinks of this water will be thirsty again, but those who drink of the water that I will give them will never be thirsty. The water that I will give will become in them a spring of water gushing up to eternal life.' The woman said to him, 'Sir, give me this water, so that I may never be thirsty or have to keep coming here to draw water.'

'Lectio divina' is simply Latin for 'spiritual reading' or 'prayerful reading'. From the beginning, Christians were advised not simply to read the Bible as a manual, a set of instructions to be put into practice, but prayerfully to immerse themselves in

Scripture. This was a natural development of Jewish spiritual and rabbinic traditions. It seems to be what Paul refers to in 1 Corinthians 2, describing the Spirit as revealing God's wisdom in people's own spirits.

In the third century, Origen described the prayerful reading of Scripture as a sacrament. The terms 'lectio divina' or 'lectio sacra' (holy reading) were in common use in major writers from this early period, such as St Ambrose and Augustine of Hippo. The best-known and earliest fully developed monastic rule for community living, written by Benedict of Nursia in 516, divides the day into a regular rhythm of times for liturgical prayer, spiritual reading, manual labour, meals and rest. Spiritual reading and manual labour are both dealt with together in Section 48 of the Benedictine Rule, defined as the two main activities with which monks should fill their time because, St Benedict began, 'idleness is an enemy of the soul'. Bernard of Clairvaux, founder of the Cistercian order in the twelfth century, considered the prayerful contemplation of Scripture, guided by the Holy Spirit, to be central to a nourishing Christian spirituality, and lectio divina was also a core element of the thirteenth-century Carmelite rule.

Lectio divina seems to have been an essentially monastic practice, taught and handed down within the monasteries by verbal instruction. Then, in the twelfth century, the first detailed description of what was entailed was published, as 'The Ladder of Monks'. This is a short essay, in the form of a letter, written by Guigo II who was Prior of the Carthusian monastery Grande Chartreuse, in southeast France. In 'The Ladder', Guigo describes in detail the methodology and purpose of this Western monastic tradition of prayerful meditation on Scripture. He sets out four steps that have been taken as the key framework of lectio divina ever since:

1. Reading;
2. Meditation;
3. Prayer;
4. Contemplation.

In modern English we often use the words 'meditation' and 'contemplation' interchangeably, and regard both as types of prayer, so it can seem strange to see these three separated out as different steps. But Guigo makes a careful, almost forensic, distinction between the purposes and practices of each stage – though he is clear that in practice they are often intermingled and don't necessarily proceed in a linear fashion.

In his own words:

> Reading is the careful study of scripture, concentrating all one's powers on it. Meditation is the busy application of the mind to seek with the help of one's own reason for knowledge of hidden truth. Prayer is the heart's devoted turning to God to drive away evil and obtain what is good. Contemplation is when the mind is in some sort lifted to God and held above itself, so that it tastes the joy of everlasting sweetness.

Contemplation, therefore, is the end goal of lectio divina. It's an awareness of God, or of some aspect of God, that you are able to rest in the presence of, drink in, and enjoy. The monastic insight is that this rarely comes naturally, and that the practice of disciplined prayerful reading can assist. Guigo is quite clear that it is perfectly possible for this contemplative awareness to be a simple gift of God's grace, given to an individual without any hard work on their part; but that is unusual. We tend to be distracted and lack focus, and the practice and structure of lectio divina therefore provide help.

We'll see in the following chapters in this second part some more specific ways in which this tradition was developed in the medieval period and beyond. But here we'll focus on the idea of a ladder. It's a deliberate reference, of course, to Jacob's dream in Genesis 28. In practising lectio divina, we consciously move from rung to rung on the four steps, with the aim of reaching a close awareness of God's presence.

Guigo refers to the passage from John's Gospel with which our chapter begins as an example of this structure happening in the Gospels. The Samaritan woman, he points out, first 'reads' (in this case, hears) the Word. She then meditates on it – that is, thinks about it deeply. She engages in discussion, even argument about it. The conversation goes on for longer than the extract quoted above; in fact, this is the longest theological discussion that the Gospels record Jesus having with any one person. She argues with him, questions him and thinks about what the Word is saying to her, using all her powers of mind. She draws her questioning from tradition, folklore, Scripture, theology and her own social and relational situation, bringing all these aspects into her dialogue with the Word.

But she doesn't stay at this purely thinking stage. She moves to prayer – 'give me this water'. In Guigo's four steps, this is what has to happen next: there will be something arising out of our thinking about the passage that makes us feel thirsty for more. When we identify that something then the time is right to move to the next stage. The prayer stage is a response to the meditation, or study, and arises out of it. Thus understood, prayer is very different from what we might be used to thinking of as prayer. It is distinct from what we might experience in our usual church services or intercession for others. Here, prayer means the step of identifying the thirst in you that your study of Scripture evokes, and consciously turning to God to ask for that particular thirst to be quenched.

The final stage, contemplation, arises out of this process. Having identified your thirst and turned to God as the source that can fill it, you move on to spend time in contemplation.

This may or may not specifically feel like God is answering your prayer. Guigo clearly expresses the hope and anticipation that sometimes lectio might end with the gift of a particular experience of or awareness of God, but this is neither necessary nor a test of whether the prayer has 'worked' or not. Often, the contemplation stage is simply about contemplating the aspect of God that the meditation and prayer stages have helped you to focus on. Contemplation is not thinking about, analysing, or mentally 'discussing' this aspect of God – that has happened at the meditation, or thinking, stage. Contemplation is simply spending time regarding this aspect of God in awe, love, reverence and/or joy.

We might take note of Guigo's analogy of eating a grape here. Reading is like popping it into your mouth; meditation is chewing on it; prayer is when you are filled with desire for more; contemplation is then taking the time to be mindfully aware of the joy and the taste and the wonder of 'grapeness'. This way of meditating on Scripture is the foundation for many of the other approaches that were developed over the medieval period, that we'll look at in the rest of this section.

Try this very simple form of lectio divina. Choose a biblical passage to read. It could be anything, but why not begin with the extract from John's Gospel that we've just been looking at? Then go through these four steps:

1. Read the passage through, slowly (or hear it read, either in a group or using a Bible recording or app). Notice a word, phrase or image that particularly strikes you. Say it out loud or write it down. Don't discuss it at this point if you're in a group – just go round, saying a word or two each without commenting on what each of the others say.

2. Now read through the passage again, with a particular awareness of the word, phrase or image that you noticed

the first time. Silently ask if there is anything more that God would like to show you about it this time.

3. Then spend some time thinking about that word, phrase or image. What resonances does it have for you? Does it make you think of other Scripture readings or of current events (in the news or in your own life)? How does it make you feel? What would you ask Jesus about it if he was sitting next to you? Do you want to agree with him, or argue with him? If you are doing this in a group, I'd suggest first spending, say, five minutes thinking about this silently. Then perhaps share your thoughts in pairs or small groups and discuss them together. Each person could then spend one minute summarising a key insight or two for the wider group.

4. Now read the passage a third time, asking God if there is a particular call to prayer for you here. Identify an aspect of your thinking and/or reading that has left you wanting more. There might be a particular thing that your meditation and discussion has left you wanting to pray for. Or it's possible that you may simply feel dissatisfaction that you don't feel you've got very far; that in itself can be a call to pray for deeper insight, or simply a symptom of the desire in you for a closer experience of God's presence. In fact, we often misdiagnose a feeling of dissatisfaction or irritability in prayer as meaning that we're not doing it very well, when it may instead be a call to a deeper encounter with God. Identify the thirst within yourself that has arisen from your meditation on the passage and ask God for what you desire. In a group, discuss this in general terms for a few minutes and then ask everyone first to write down, privately, what they want to ask God for (which helps people to put it into words), and then to close their eyes and say that to God.

5. Finally, spend a few minutes in silence, contemplating the aspect of God that your reading, meditation and prayer

have led you to be aware of. Don't worry about trying to do this well, simply sit in silence with your focus on just being aware, in this moment, of what your reading, thinking and prayer have led you to.

Try this, for example, with John 15:1–8, Philippians 2:1–11 or 1 John 1:1–9.

9

Medieval fourfold interpretation

Read: Isaiah 10:33–11:1

> Look, the Sovereign, the LORD of hosts,
>   will lop the boughs with terrifying power;
>   the tallest trees will be cut down,
>   and the lofty will be brought low.
> He will hack down the thickets of the forest with an axe,
>   and Lebanon with its majestic trees will fall.
> A shoot shall come out from the stock of Jesse,
>   and a branch shall grow out of his roots.

It was as clear to medieval Christian preachers, scholars and writers as it is to us today that not everything in Scripture is immediately or obviously edifying. Early Christians saw perfectly clearly that the Bible contains all sort of episodes and stories that seem incompatible with Jesus' message of love. They, like us, were troubled that it abounds with examples of bad behaviour that surely God can't intend us to copy: bloodthirsty genocide, rulers and petty officials abusing their power, jealousy, lust, violence, injustice. It contains references to God destroying people and civilisations, as in the Isaiah reading above. And much of what it describes can seem, on a superficial or literal reading, to be either ridiculous (imagining God as a woodcutter) or of merely historical or antiquarian record (why should they, or we, care if Lebanon fell, thousands of years ago?). These were criticisms that the intelligentsia of their day frequently levelled at the early church, mocking its reliance on an ancient set of stories about the troubled history of a relatively obscure nation on the fringes of the Roman Empire.

The question early theologians had to struggle with, therefore, was how they were to reconcile the existence of such stories in the Bible with their conviction, and the biblical witness itself, that God speaks through the Bible, and that it was written for our edification.

It was in pondering this question that the idea developed of a fourfold approach to the interpretation of Scripture. Some passages could be read simply, at face value. Others might need deeper layers of meaning to be uncovered in order for them to be nourishing for the faith and life of the reader, or of those hearing a preacher's words. And even passages that were immediately satisfying and nourishing might have hidden depths – they might communicate God's love to us on more than one level. The task of a preacher, in particular, was to study and digest a passage so that they could help others to find as much nourishment as possible in it. Food imagery, often surprisingly graphic to modern ears, was frequently used; medieval writers might imagine prayerful contemplation in terms of being breast-fed by the Virgin Mary, or even, in a gender-bending image, by the maternal breasts of Jesus; or they might speak of sucking the marrow from the bones, or of bees greedy to gather as much nectar as possible from the flowers that surrounded them.

In other words, the biblical texts were understood to be full of meaning, some brimming over and obvious, some hidden beneath the surface and requiring concentrated sucking or chewing to extract it. This was not seen as a limitation of or problem with Scripture, but as further evidence, if any were needed, of its unique status as a divinely inspired text. God, as co-author with the various human writers, could ensure that there was more meaning to a text than even the original human author may have been aware of at the time of writing.

The four 'layers' of meaning that developed as standard over the medieval period were:

1. The *literal* or plain sense – What the words actually said, including how they would have been understood in their original context.
2. The *allegorical*, illustrative or doctrinal sense – What the text might tell us about the Church and Christian belief.
3. The *tropological*, moral or soul sense – How this applies to our inner moral and spiritual lives.
4. The *anagogical* or future vision sense – How the passage points to the future, to hope in the afterlife or to the ultimate destiny of humanity.

For the early Church Fathers, allegory was a way of seeking christological or other doctrinal truths in parts of Scripture that would otherwise simply be irrelevant, and sometimes rather unpleasant, ancient history. Some of these ways of reading elements of the Old Testament have become so familiar to us over the centuries that we rarely stop to question them. For example, many of us will have heard Isaiah 11:1 ('a shoot will come up from the stump of Jesse') read at countless Christmas carol services, and the idea of reading this as a prophecy of Jesus seems obvious and familiar.

On the other hand, some of these medieval interpretations can seem very strange or fanciful to us today. It's important to note that, for all the serious scholars of the time, the literal meaning always came first and was always foundational for the other three layers. That is, the literal meaning of the passage – what the story actually says – had to shape and direct any thinking, meditation and prayerful contemplation that might lead you to other layers of meaning. Giving weight to the literal meaning did not suggest that a passage had to be taken literally (that we were actually to imagine God as a woodcutter in Isaiah 10); it was about taking seriously the imagery and intention of the passage (see the following chapter).

It's also important to note that not all passages were assumed to contain all four layers of meaning, nor were the four types of interpretation seen as progressive. One common misconception today, as Eastern ideas of 'higher consciousness' have permeated into society, is that these four types of interpretation were about a spiritual elite progressing through them, with later 'stages' being superior and inaccessible to beginners. But this is a distortion: all texts were assumed to have a literal meaning, while some may, in addition, admit one or more of the other types of interpretation. It was not assumed that all passages had all four types of meaning but simply that they might do, and it was worth thinking about. The three types of interpretation beyond the literal were to be looked for especially in those cases when the literal meaning seemed baffling or absurd.

The underlying assumption of this school of thought was that the Bible is meant to nourish us in faith, so when we read something that doesn't immediately obviously do that, there must be more to the passage than first meets the eye.

Allegorical interpretation is often used as an umbrella term for all of the last three methods; they are all approached in a similar way but focus on three different areas of interest or application. The following chapters will explore in more detail how you might go about reading the Bible seeking some of these potential layers of meaning, and will outline some of the guidelines that early church theologians gave to prevent some of the wildest flights of fancy that allegory could be used for.

I'd suggest reading the next three chapters in conjunction with this one. But the simple idea to take away is that, where the meaning of a passage seems on the face of it to be toxic rather than nourishing, try looking for as many of these layers of meaning as possible.

To have a go at this, first divide a piece of paper into four quarters. In each quarter, brainstorm what the possible range of meanings might be for this passage: on a literal level in the first quarter; as a metaphor or allegory for Church doctrines in the second; as an allegory or symbol for something in our inner moral or spiritual lives in the third; and similarly for ideas about the future, or the Christian hope, in the fourth.

The key with brainstorming is to write down anything you think of and not to make judgements about how 'good' or 'right' your ideas are at this stage. You might consider any similarities in words or images to other Bible stories; compare and contrast the moral or doctrinal perspective of the passage with others you know, either from the Bible or elsewhere; or think about associations with art, literature or film. If you are doing this in a group, you could have a large flipchart or four areas of wall for the four sections, and invite people to write down each idea they have on a sticky note, and add it to the communal list of ideas. If ideas stop flowing, read the passage over again, and invite yourself and others to be as creative as possible in your responses.

Then, when plenty of ideas have been generated, begin the process of assessment. Start by spending some time reading over the different ideas that you have generated. Which feel most positive? Which feel 'edifying', or nourishing? Circle these on your sheet. In a group, you could give each person a set of small sticky dots, or a different coloured pen, and invite them to add

62

a dot or a star next to the ideas that they find nourishing for faith. Which quadrant has most circles, dots or stars?

Finally, remove the sticky notes without dots or stars, or if you are doing this alone redraw your quarters and just write in the ideas that you circled. Spend some time as a group discussing, or on your own contemplating, the points that you have identified.

Try doing this, for example, with Genesis 21:1–20, Judges 19: 16–30, Matthew 2:1–12 or Mark 1:1–13.

10

Literal interpretation

Read: Genesis 1:1-5

> In the beginning when God created the heavens and the earth,
> the earth was a formless void and darkness covered the face
> of the deep, while a wind from God swept over the face of
> the waters. Then God said, 'Let there be light'; and there was
> light. And God saw that the light was good; and God separated
> the light from the darkness. God called the light Day, and the
> darkness he called Night. And there was evening and there was
> morning, the first day.

As we've seen, the literal meaning of the text doesn't mean
taking the text literally. That is, it didn't mean, for early or
medieval Bible scholars, the kind of biblical fundamentalism that 'taking the Bible literally' can imply to us now. It
didn't mean that a medieval reader would have assumed that
everything recorded in the Bible actually happened in history
exactly as described, or that it was directly dictated by God
without any shaping or contribution by a human author or
editor. Much of what contemporary biblical scholars would
think of as historical, contextual or literary readings – contrasted with a fundamentalist, 'literal' approach to Scripture
– were included by medieval scholars in their conception of a
literal understanding.

This passage from the very beginning of the Bible provides a good example. We can hardly fail to be aware nowadays of creationism – the fundamentalist belief that the Genesis account of creation must be literally true because it is in the Bible – and that this is a litmus test for whether you are a 'Bible believing Christian' or not. Even those who find this impossible to believe often assume that creationists are right in thinking that they are in line with the vast majority of historical Christians until the Enlightenment, and that reading the Genesis account of creation as more than a description of actual historical events is a very modern development in Christian thought. However, this is very far from the truth.

The early Church Fathers assumed that a literal interpretation of such passages was an impoverished one. One of my favourite early church quotations is from the fourth section of Origen's *De Principiis*. It is startling if you've been used to thinking that everyone before the Enlightenment took the Bible literally:

> Who that has understanding will suppose that the first, and second, and third day, with evening and morning, existed without a sun, and moon, and stars? ... And who is so foolish as to suppose that God, like a farmer, planted a paradise in Eden, towards the east, and placed in it a tree of life, visible and palpable, so that one tasting of the fruit by the bodily teeth obtained life? ... And if God is said to walk in the paradise in the evening, and Adam to hide himself under a tree, I do not suppose that anyone doubts that these things figuratively indicate certain mysteries, the history having taken place in appearance, and not literally.

This was not limited to the ancient texts of the Old Testament. Origen was clear that the Gospels, too, are full of the same kind of stories. For example, the story of the devil leading Jesus to a high place to see all the kingdoms of the world cannot possibly be literally true – there is nobody who could take seriously the idea that a real vantage point exists from which you could see all the known kingdoms. So, Origen concludes, 'the attentive reader may notice in the Gospels innumerable other passages like these, and be convinced that in the histories that are literally recorded, circumstances that did not occur are inserted'.

This passage from Genesis 1 is also discussed by Augustine of Hippo, a North African writer and bishop whose writings were hugely influential in the development of Western Christian thought. He uses this passage as an example to discuss how to read the Bible and what it means to read it literally and seriously.

Augustine begins Book 12 of his *Confessions* by discussing what we would now call semiotics – the theory of signs. Words, he explains, are a kind of sign, at least twice removed from the thing that they signify. A written word (the marks we see on the page) is a sign of the spoken word, or the word that was in the original author's mind, but that word itself is in turn merely a sign indicating the speaker's or writer's thoughts. Augustine was contributing to a debate that was going on at the time about whether the true, or truest, meaning of a scriptural passage was the author's intention, or whether what the words mean to us as we read them now is more important. It's a familiar debate today, as we ask whether what the words would have meant in their original context is different from what they might mean to us now, and which of those meanings, if different, is the 'real' or most important meaning.

Augustine points out that we only have the words on the page to go on. We don't, and can't, have access to what an author was originally thinking; we only have the signs that have been handed down to us. In particular, Augustine argues that because Scripture is co-authored by a human writer and by

God the human authorial intention can't be the only or most important thing. A text, therefore, might have been thought by the original author to mean one thing, but the Holy Spirit, as co-author, might guide us to read it in a way that would have been a complete surprise to the original author. Similarly, people in the future might be guided by God to see something different in the text from that which Augustine sees.

Signs can have multiple meanings, so they admit a range of understandings. That doesn't mean that we can just make up any meaning for a text – but it does mean that we should explore the full spectrum of meaning that each word-sign has in order to explore the full meaning of the text. Several meanings will almost always be equally, literally true. As Augustine says, we should aim to look for 'such abundance of most true meanings, as may be extracted out of those words'.

Using the example of those opening words of Genesis, Augustine directly addresses the limitations of what we might now call a 'literal' reading. Some people, he says, when they read or hear these words, will take them very literally indeed. They will imagine God as a 'thing', existing in space and time, like an extremely powerful person; they will imagine too that if you were there you'd have heard actual words spoken, and then would have seen actual matter coming into being. For them, this literal reading of the words is like a nest, cradling a fledgling faith. It's not to be despised, but it is not getting full value from the words. A more mature faith will go further. In this exuberant image: 'others, unto whom these words are no longer a nest, but deep shady fruit-bowers, see the fruits concealed therein, fly joyously around, and with cheerful notes seek out, and pluck them'.

So, for example, some readers, focusing on the phrase 'in the beginning', might see it as a point in time, but others might read it differently. Augustine suggests that it could be read as referring to God's Wisdom – 'in God's wisdom, God created heaven and earth'— rather than to an actual moment in time. Someone else might read it and be struck by a fresh awareness that all that is, now as well as in the past, is the product of God's will, and that all the diversity we see around us is therefore beautiful. You might, in contemplating the idea of a beginning, be drawn into a fresh sense of awe at God's eternity. And as we dwell more on different aspects of the passage, other insights will emerge. Again, these will be different in different people. The limited words that we read on the page, Augustine suggests, are like the depths of water in the narrow channel of a river's source at its spring. The meaning is all contained in those few, narrow words; but further downstream, it splits into many different channels, streams and rivers, as different people interpret and read it, and different places are irrigated by it. 'In this diversity of the true opinions,' Augustine concludes, 'let Truth herself produce concord.' It is of ultimate importance to Augustine that we don't use the fact that we each see different things in the text as a source of division, but let the rich diversity of interpretations give us even more reason to love God and our neighbour. We'll look more at Augustine's emphasis on love as an interpretative principle in chapter 13.

A literal reading, then, in this fourfold approach involves detailed study of the passage. It involves asking questions about the original context and authorship, and what these words might have meant to earlier generations of readers. It involves understanding the full implications of any images, numbers, objects, political or geographical references. Medieval interpreters rejoiced in such multiplicity of meanings and saw such implications and resonances as part of the literal meaning of the text. Numbers and numerology were also given great significance, in a way that can seem very alien to us, for whom these concepts do not feature in our usual reading toolkit.

So the literal meaning, which was foundational for any of the other three, really meant much of what we might call study today. It could involve research, including questions of translation and language. It drew heavily on the readers' knowledge of other biblical texts, so that resonances and parallels could be fully appreciated as part of the range of meaning. And the fruits of this study, the images, resonances, cross-references and questions that it produced, were then used as the raw material for a second, third and even fourth round of reading, in the hope and expectation that the text would continue to yield more nectar to an eager, faithful reader.

II

Allegory

Read: Matthew 20:1–16

For the kingdom of heaven is like a landowner who went out early in the morning to hire labourers for his vineyard. After agreeing with the labourers for the usual daily wage, he sent them into his vineyard. When he went out about nine o'clock, he saw others standing idle in the market-place; and he said to them, 'You also go into the vineyard, and I will pay you whatever is right.' So they went. When he went out again about noon and about three o'clock, he did the same. And about five o'clock he went out and found others standing around; and he said to them, 'Why are you standing here idle all day?' They said to him, 'Because no one has hired us.' He said to them, 'You also go into the vineyard.' When evening came, the owner of the vineyard said to his manager, 'Call the labourers and give them their pay, beginning with the last and then going to the first.' When those hired about five o'clock came, each of them received the usual daily wage. Now when the first came, they thought they would receive more; but each of them also received the usual daily wage. And when they received it, they grumbled against the landowner, saying, 'These last worked only one hour, and you have made them equal to us who have borne the burden of the day and the scorching heat.' But he replied to one of them, 'Friend, I am doing you no wrong; did you not agree with me for the usual daily wage? Take what belongs to you and go; I choose to give to this last the same as I give to you. Am I not allowed to do what I choose with what belongs to me? Or are you envious because I am generous?' So the last will be first, and the first will be last.

As we've discovered, allegorical interpretation of the Scriptures was a very early development in Christian theology. It was in many ways a natural development from Jewish midrashic traditions of interpretation. These assumed first, that the text was always relevant now, and second, that it was always to some extent cryptic and in need of skilled interpretation to draw out its meaning. Jesus' extensive use of puzzling parables gave credence to this view. Parables are clearly stories that invite further thought; they invite the reader or hearer to ponder what the deeper implications of the story might be.

In an allegorical reading it is assumed that people, places and things refer to more than just their own reality within the story; they tell us something about God, faith or the spiritual life. The early Church Fathers were quite clear that this was essential to reading the Old Testament, which would otherwise, they said, be of merely antiquarian interest as the history of a particular tribe in the ancient Near East. As we noted in chapter 9, this was partly a reaction to intellectual critiques of the time, and partly a theological response to the problem that the meaning of many of the stories of the Old Testament were not, on the face of it, immediately of obvious spiritual value. You may well have heard, or said yourself, something similar nowadays. People quite often say to me that they like Jesus and the God of the New Testament, but find it hard to reconcile that God of love with the punitive violence of many of the Old Testament texts.

In response to these critiques, early theologians concluded that, if a scriptural passage seemed at face value to be inconsistent with Christian teaching, then it must have an allegorical meaning. In an allegorical reading, every apparently random detail of the story might be significant, as a 'type', a symbol or parallel with a spiritual truth that God wants to teach us through the passage. As the early third-century theologian Origen put it, 'material things are types of spiritual things, and historical events of intelligible realities'.

Allegorical readings had a particular focus on Christian doctrine, which was used as the interpretative key to passages that seemed obscure. If they weren't immediately edifying, then they must be allegories for some part or other of the teaching of the Church. This way of reading was, of course, to some extent a circular argument: the Bible had given the Church its doctrine, and now must be interpreted in line with that. In some cases, it was criticised, even by other early church theologians, for not taking the original Jewish context of the Hebrew Scriptures seriously enough. For example, water was almost always seen as a symbol of Christian baptism, and so key episodes in the Hebrew Scriptures like Noah's flood, or the crossing of the Red Sea, tended to be interpreted almost exclusively as types of Christian baptism to the neglect of their meaning in Jewish spirituality, culture and self-understanding. The excesses and flights of fancy of allegorical understandings could get ridiculous – not just to modern ears but to many of their contemporaries as well. St Basil, for example, dismissed the tendency to allegorise in his *Hexaemeron*:

> There are those truly, who do not admit the common sense of the Scriptures, for whom water is not water, but some other nature, who see in a plant, in a fish, what their fancy wishes, who change the nature of reptiles and of wild beasts to suit their allegories, like the interpreters of dreams who explain visions in sleep to make them serve their own ends. For me grass is grass; plant, fish, wild beast, domestic animal, I take all in the literal sense.

For most interpreters, though, it was assumed that allegory provided an additional layer of meaning to some stories even when they had a literal meaning too, or that it provided a way of interpreting stories that made little religious sense at the literal level.

The parable of the workers in the vineyard is an example of a puzzling story that has had many different allegorical interpretations and still has the capacity to infuriate a modern congregation. We have an instinctive sense of fair play that leads many people to consider that, however generous this was of the employer, the people who had worked all day were justified in being angry and resentful. Every time I have preached on this passage, I've encountered anger and incredulity from those hearing this story for the first time. Their anger springs from a real passion for justice and, often, from an awareness of the realities of exploitation and a sense of helplessness in the face of arbitrary and unfair decisions by employers. This is still, therefore, a story that does not seem immediately helpful. What can an allegorical reading contribute to our understanding of it?

A simple example of an allegorical interpretation of this parable is given by Irenaeus, writing in the second half of the second century. In his book *Against Heresies*, Irenaeus argued that the parable shows the continuity between the God of the Jews and the God of the Christians. The 'day' of the parable represents the whole of known time. God calls some people at the beginning, at creation, in the Genesis narrative. Others are called at various times later, over the long history of the Old Testament, and others are called in recent times, by Jesus and the Christian Church. There is therefore only one God – the owner of the vineyard – and despite different people being called to work at different times and under different conditions, all will have the same reward.

More complex allegorical interpretations followed. For Origen, the parable could be interpreted as an allegory for individual salvation, with the 'day' referring to the span of a human life. Some are called at the beginning of the day, in infant baptism, others in their youths, as adults, in old age or even on their deathbeds. The time translated in our reading above as 'about five in the afternoon' is literally 'at the eleventh hour'; the colloquial English usage of the phrase as meaning 'just in time' preserves the ancient interpretation of this parable. On this reading of the text, it doesn't matter whether you have served God all your life or are a last-minute convert, your (heavenly) reward is the same. An alternative perspective from the fourteenth century applies the parable to death in infancy, comforting bereaved parents that no matter how short the time their children served God on earth, their reward in heaven will be no less than if they'd lived a long and devout life.

In a sermon on this parable, Augustine of Hippo combines all these interpretations and adds some further elaboration. He begins by taking the idea of a spiritual harvest further, describing God as cultivating us, planting the seed of his Word in our hearts and 'by the plough of his Word' seeking to root out sin so that the fruit of piety can grow and be gathered in. God rejoices in a good spiritual harvest, works hard for it, and expects fruit from it. After giving both the allegorical interpretations above, Augustine then turns to two potential objections. First, why should we bother to answer the call to go and work earlier in our lives if we can get the same reward from a deathbed conversion? He points out that we don't know when our deaths will come, so we might believe we are being called in the heat of the day but it might in fact be the eleventh hour for us. Second, Augustine asks, what if you don't feel that God has come to call you? This is exactly the point that someone made in one of my churches recently when we were discussing this passage. Asked who we each identified with in the story, she said that she felt she was still in the market place, feeling left behind and unwanted. In the context of his sermon, Augustine says – well, this is the call! The fact that you are hearing or reading this now is the vineyard owner sending one of his servants to come and ask you to join in the work. The denarius is being offered to you here and now – will you accept it?

This approach to the Bible takes the Christian understanding of doctrine as foundational for interpretation. If the passage that you are reading seems inconsistent with Christian teaching, look for a symbolic meaning. Although allegory is out of fashion nowadays, many of the standard readings of Scripture that we are familiar with are, in fact, fundamentally allegorical in nature. This way of reading permits an element of playfulness. Try listing as many possible allegorical readings of a passage as you can think of, either alone or in a group – as far-fetched as you like. They will not, of course, all be 'right' or even plausible, but you may well find that in that playfulness you are surprised by some fresh insight into the range of meanings of the text. Try this, for example, with Song of Songs 1:1–7, Isaiah 5:1–10 or Revelation 22:1–5.

12

The inner life

Read: Luke 10:25–37

Just then a lawyer stood up to test Jesus. 'Teacher,' he said, 'what must I do to inherit eternal life?' He said to him, 'What is written in the law? What do you read there?' He answered, 'You shall love the Lord your God with all your heart, and with all your soul, and with all your strength, and with all your mind; and your neighbour as yourself.' And he said to him, 'You have given the right answer; do this, and you will live.'

But wanting to justify himself, he asked Jesus, 'And who is my neighbour?' Jesus replied, 'A man was going down from Jerusalem to Jericho, and fell into the hands of robbers, who stripped him, beat him, and went away, leaving him half dead. Now by chance a priest was going down that road; and when he saw him, he passed by on the other side. So likewise a Levite, when he came to the place and saw him, passed by on the other side. But a Samaritan while travelling came near him; and when he saw him, he was moved with pity. He went to him and bandaged his wounds, having poured oil and wine on them. Then he put him on his own animal, brought him to an inn, and took care of him. The next day he took out two denarii, gave them to the innkeeper, and said, "Take care of him; and when I come back, I will repay you whatever more you

spend." Which of these three, do you think, was a neighbour to the man who fell into the hands of the robbers?' He
said, 'The one who showed him mercy.' Jesus said to him,
'Go and do likewise.'

This chapter focuses on the third layer of the medieval four-
fold interpretation of Scripture, the tropological, moral or
'soul' meaning, which uses a similar allegorical approach to
that outlined in the previous chapter, but specifically applies it
to considering what the passage might mean in our own inner
and spiritual lives, rather than for Christian doctrine. This
shouldn't be confused with simply reading the literal meaning
of the text and seeking its *application* to our lives. Instead, this
approach takes the imagery and questions that emerge from a
detailed study of the text and asks how they might shed light
on our inner moral and spiritual lives. Remember: the allegorical approach asks how these images, details and questions
might illuminate the world of doctrinal faith and/or the life of
the Church, while the fourth, anagogical reading (which we
won't go into further in this book to avoid repetition, as the
technique is substantially the same as the allegorical) asks what
light they might shed on questions of our ultimate destiny or
Christian hope.

Reading the Bible in relation to our own moral and spiritual
development has had a resurgence in recent years and is known
as an 'inner life' reading. In approaching the Bible like this,
we start with the literal meaning and then abstract it slightly.
What questions does the passage throw up? What moods or
emotions does it evoke, what challenges does it pose, what
images does it invite us to dwell on? The next stage is to ask
the same questions (or pose the same challenges, see what is
reflected by the same images, as appropriate) of our inner life.
What might correspond to the various elements of the story in
your inner life?

Parables are particularly appropriate for this kind of reading, as they are so clearly meant to be read on multiple levels, and to provoke strong emotional responses for you to chew over. The literal meaning of the parable of the good Samaritan clearly isn't that there really was a traveller, a road, some robbers, and so on. Asking what was 'really' going on in the mind of the priest, the Samaritan or the robbers is not literal reading. Taking the Bible literally, in the case of the parables, means hearing and understanding them *as (fictional) stories*, and taking seriously their historical context, the way they may have been heard by various groups, and so on. An inner life reading starts with this literal analysis, and then takes it inside.

On a literal level, this parable is an answer, and perhaps a rebuke, to the question 'Who is my neighbour?' Reading it at a literal level challenges us to reconsider our negative stereotypes of those we reject as unable or unlikely sources of help. It's useful to know something of the context: that Samaritans and Jews were local political and religious enemies, and that tensions between the two groups were running particularly high at this time. It may also help to know that the road from Jerusalem to Jericho was notorious for bandits, and that it wasn't unknown for bandits to use seemingly injured accomplices as bait to lure unwary travellers into an ambush. Or that priests and Levites followed particular religious laws in which dead bodies could make you ritually unclean. It may help to know that Jerusalem wasn't just another city in the Jewish worldview, but was the home of the (singular) temple, the place that symbolised God's presence with them as a nation.

All of this, to the medieval mind, is part of the literal meaning of the text and enriches our understanding of it. And this literal reading of the story is foundational to an inner life reading, which is shaped by it and the questions it poses. In the allegorical approach, things, people and places were considered as symbols for elements of Christian doctrine. Here they are considered as symbols for elements of our inner moral and spiritual lives.

So, for example, in reflecting on this passage I might ask myself questions like these:

- What journey am I on – either now or generally? If Jerusalem represents the City of God, what tasks or journeys do I feel called to pursue that I believe are worth leaving that for? Or what journey do I feel I have to undertake alone? What journey do I feel particularly vulnerable on at the moment?
- What in my life robs me of the things I value? What robs me, or threatens to rob me, of my health and/or my ability to complete my plans under my own steam? Or what in my life has wounded me so deeply that when I think about it I am left half-dead and unable to function effectively?
- What part of myself do I despise, reject and certainly don't expect to be helpful to me? What is the least likely part of my character or psychological make up to be able to help?
- What does it feel like to imagine that despised part of me coming along and meeting me in my woundedness? What does it feel like, in my imagination, to let that despised part of myself take charge of this next part of my journey? How does it feel to let myself be carried along by that part of myself and cared for by it, for a time?
- What parts of myself or my inner life have I expected to help in my woundedness, only to find that they don't touch the pain?

This is a way of reading that demands a bit more time and mental energy of you than some others, so don't attempt it when you are rushed for time or can't get some mental space. Ideally, block out an hour when you can go somewhere quiet and be undisturbed. It may help for you to have a notebook and pencil with you. Turn your phone off, shut the door and begin by asking God to guide your prayerful reading of the passage.

First read the passage you've chosen through two or three times, noting the literal meaning and the questions or challenges that the text throws up for you at a literal level. Scribble these down, probing for more layers of literal meaning: you might try thinking about each of the characters in the story in turn, and each physical location, to draw out as much literal meaning as possible. What would you imagine a preacher telling you about this passage? How does it make you feel?

Then begin to ask the questions that the passage has thrown up for you of your inner life. What if each of the characters is a part of you – which part of you would be represented by each one? What about the locations or objects in the story – what could each of them symbolise to you in your inner life, today?

It is often helpful to end by going and making a cup of tea and then returning to your quiet place and noting down, in your notebook or journal, any insights that you have had or questions that you are left with.

Try this with other parables such as Matthew 13:24–30, Luke 12:15–21, Luke 14:7–11. You could also try it with episodes from the Gospels such as Luke 9:28–35 or John 6:1–14.

13

Augustine's rule of love

Read: 1 Corinthians 13

If I speak in the tongues of mortals and of angels, but do not have love, I am a noisy gong or a clanging cymbal. And if I have prophetic powers, and understand all mysteries and all knowledge, and if I have all faith, so as to remove mountains, but do not have love, I am nothing. If I give away all my possessions, and if I hand over my body so that I may boast, but do not have love, I gain nothing.

Love is patient; love is kind; love is not envious or boastful or arrogant or rude. It does not insist on its own way; it is not irritable or resentful; it does not rejoice in wrongdoing, but rejoices in the truth. It bears all things, believes all things, hopes all things, endures all things. Love never ends. But as for prophecies, they will come to an end; as for tongues, they will cease; as for knowledge, it will come to an end. For we know only in part, and we prophesy only in part; but when the complete comes, the partial will come to an end. When I was a child, I spoke like a child, I thought like a child, I reasoned like a child; when I became an adult, I put an end to childish ways. For now we see in a mirror, dimly, but then we will see face to face. Now I know only in part; then I will know fully, even as I have been fully known. And now faith, hope, and love abide, these three; and the greatest of these is love.

Augustine of Hippo, writing at the end of the fourth century and early fifth century, took as read the understanding that some parts of the Bible were to be interpreted literally and others allegorically (he used the term 'figuratively'). But Augustine added to the tradition a new guiding principle – love. 'The love of God for His own sake, and the love of our neighbour for God's sake, is the fulfilment and end of all Scripture,' he wrote, summarising the argument of Book 1 of his *On Christian Teaching*. And 'Faith, hope and love are graces essentially necessary' for anyone wishing to understand and explain Scripture.

You may have seen some version of these words that have been circulating on the internet for some years now: 'God created people to be loved, and things to be used. The problem now is that things are being loved, and people used.' This is not quite the language that Augustine would have employed, but it neatly encapsulates something of his approach. For Augustine, God was to be 'enjoyed'. Indeed, the aim of human life was to enjoy God. Enjoyment of all the good things in creation – our own bodies, food, drink, the beauties of nature, science and so on – used rightly, could help us to reach this place of loving God. And this included loving other people, because we are all made in God's image. Augustine calls this Charity. On the other hand, there is always a temptation to love turned away from rather than in the direction of God. Augustine called this Lust –the wrong use of creation, seeking to use things and other people purely for our own pleasure, rather than with a view to loving God. Although nowadays the word 'lust' is rather unhelpfully associated specifically with sexual desire, for Augustine it meant something more like greed. It was the desire to possess and use people and things rather than loving them. For Augustine, this was the great choice that humanity was faced with.

There were several elements to the way in which Augustine applied his rule of love in biblical interpretation. First, it provided the principle for deciding whether a particular passage was to be interpreted literally or called for a figurative interpretation. We've already seen that for early church theologians it was standard practice to apply an allegorical reading to any passage that wasn't obviously edifying at a literal level. For Augustine, the question was simple. Did the literal meaning of any scriptural text tend to produce love for God and one's neighbour? If it did, then the literal meaning sufficed and there was no benefit to searching for an allegorical meaning. If it did not, then a figurative reading must be required.

This approach deals very simply with the objection that the Bible contains many stories that we find hard to believe can really be what God wants for the world. As we've seen, it can be easy nowadays for us to think that such objections are a very modern phenomenon, and that everyone in the past had no problem taking the Bible literally. It is striking, then, that Augustine deals with a whole series of such objections. What if a passage shows God behaving violently or harshly? What if a story describes someone who is held up as a saint, a hero of the faith, behaving badly, or saying something that seems simply unacceptable to us? What about commands, prohibitions or customs that seem only relevant in their own particular historical context? These are not new questions and Augustine takes them seriously as genuine objections that need to be addressed. And he applies the rule of love to each of them in turn. In Chapter 12 of Book 3 of *On Christian Teaching*, he puts it most clearly:

Those things, again, whether only saying or whether actual deeds, which appear to the inexperienced to be sinful and which are ascribed to God, or to men whose holiness is put before us as an example, are wholly figurative, and the hidden kernel of meaning they contain is to be picked out as food for the nourishment of charity.

Following on from this, Augustine was clear that the test of any interpretation was whether it built up love for God and/or neighbour. If an interpretation did this, it was a good one; if it did not, it was a bad one. This was not wishy-washy liberal thinking; Augustine's works contain a forensic level of analysis of what exactly love is, and how easy it is for us to twist its definition to our own ends. He also gave detailed instructions on other guidelines to help in interpretation, and commended serious study of philosophy, science, history and languages. Augustine was clear that study of rhetoric and grammar were very helpful in enabling us to see that a particular figure of speech might be metaphorical, or ironical, rather than necessarily being meant literally; and he insisted that interpretations of obscure passages should be grounded by a 'fact check' against the more obvious parts of the Bible. But ultimately, as in 1 Corinthians 13, all the knowledge in the world was useless if a reading wasn't grounded in love and didn't promote love.

So important was this principle that Augustine was even clear that an interpretation could be wildly wrong (based, for example, on an inaccurate translation or a misunderstanding of the historical context) but nevertheless wasn't a serious mistake if it built up love. Love as a destination is more important than the road taken to get there. Augustine even went so far as to say that if you got to the destination of love by leaving the 'high road' of Scripture all together, like someone taking a detour across fields rather than following the path, that was acceptable, providing you arrived at the same place. It wasn't advisable to train people in this because there was a danger that, if they got into the habit of thinking they didn't need the road map of Scripture, they would get lost on future occasions;

but what ultimately mattered was getting to the right destination – love. For Augustine the Scriptures, like all of creation, are in essence simply tools – wonderful, inspired tools, but tools none the less – that God has provided to help us make the journey to love.

This is more of an underlying attitude to Scripture than a technique to be applied, but it is worth trying to hold onto when you read any part of the Bible. The simple question to ask yourself is: Does this passage, on the face of it, increase my love of God and of God in other people?

If the answer is yes, then spend some time dwelling on a particular aspect that the passage has opened up for you. Is there a habit of greed, or lust, of misusing people or things, that the reading challenges you about? Is there a particular aspect of God that it helps you to 'enjoy' or contemplate?

If the answer is no, then think about how it might be interpreted figuratively in a way that *would* increase love. Is there a specific aspect of sin that the passage warns about? Augustine would particularly encourage you to consider this if the passage contains violent imagery, and especially violence ascribed to God; what might, figuratively speaking, be being violently rejected here? Consider rhetorical devices that might be being used; could the passage be meant to be read, for example, in an ironic or sarcastic tone of voice? If a story about a person is offensive or distasteful, might that encourage us to be humble about our own capacity for sin or self-deception?

14

Ignatian imagination

Read: Mark 10:46—51

> They came to Jericho. As he and his disciples and a large crowd
> were leaving Jericho, Bartimaeus son of Timaeus, a blind beg-
> gar, was sitting by the roadside. When he heard that it was
> Jesus of Nazareth, he began to shout out and say, 'Jesus, Son
> of David, have mercy on me!' Many sternly ordered him to be
> quiet, but he cried out even more loudly, 'Son of David, have
> mercy on me!' Jesus stood still and said, 'Call him here.' And
> they called the blind man, saying to him, 'Take heart; get up,
> he is calling you.' So throwing off his cloak, he sprang up and
> came to Jesus. Then Jesus said to him, 'What do you want me
> to do for you?'

Imagining yourself into a Gospel scene was one of the most popular medieval approaches to reading the Bible. Nowadays, it is
most associated with the Spiritual Exercises of Ignatius of Loy-
ola, who founded the Jesuit order and whose Exercises still form
the basis of much spiritual direction today. Ignatius was an active
young nobleman in the early fifteenth century, a soldier and man-
about-town, who in his youth was fired up by chivalric romances.
When he was badly injured in a battle, and convalescing in a family castle, he found that daydreaming about his favourite tales of
chivalry left him feeling depressed and dissatisfied. There were

few books available to read, so he found himself reading the *Vita Christi*, or *Life of Christ*, by Ludolph of Saxony. This retold episodes from Jesus' life from the Gospels and encouraged the reader to meditate on them, imagining themselves at the scene – imagining, for example, that you are one of the visitors to the nativity or a bystander at the crucifixion.

Originally published in 1374, the *Vita Christi* was hugely popular across medieval Europe, with over two hundred manuscript copies still surviving today. It often surprises people to realise that such works of popular devotion were in far wider circulation than actual Bibles in the medieval period; it's notable that it was this book, rather than the Bible itself, that was available to inspire Ignatius in his long convalescence. Ludolph's book was itself based on an earlier work, *Meditations on the Life of Christ*, attributed to St Bonaventure, which had circulated since around 1300. This again was a bestseller of its day, and its English translation in 1410 seems to have been the most popular new piece of literature to have been published in fifteenth-century England.

So when Ignatius found himself reading Ludolph of Saxony's *Life of Christ*, he was reading a bestseller, a spiritual classic. And when he put it into practice for himself, he was struck first of all by the similarity with his daydreaming about the chivalric romances that he had loved. He had had plenty of practice at imagining himself into a story and daydreaming about what part he himself would play in the tale. The insight that changed Ignatius' life, and developed into what was to become the Spiritual Exercises, was that when he read these stories, and found himself daydreaming over them, the after-effects were very different. Imagining himself in the Gospel stories – even if the actual story wasn't very exciting – left him with a lingering sense of consolation, while imagining himself as a chivalric hero, though hugely enjoyable at the time, often left him feeling depressed and empty.

Ignatius developed a method for getting the most out of the experience of imaginative meditation. In the formal Exercises, this is done in a structured way alongside an experienced spiritual director, but it is also immediately accessible to everyone. It is well worth giving it a try, and may particularly suit you if you are someone who often dreams or daydreams in full colour. There are three parts to this approach. Although the core of it, the imaginative meditation itself, is central and can stand alone, the Ignatian method adds the preparation and review stages. which are worth giving time to; they are designed to ensure that you get the most out of the meditation. The review, in particular, is a stage so easily skipped, especially if you don't feel that your meditation has been much of a success. Yet it is often in the review stage, rather than in the meditation itself, that the insights, the 'consolations' in Ignatius' language, are realised. In my journal, the review section often begins 'That was a bit rubbish, I'm not very good at this' and ends 'Oh. Wow! Thanks.' So don't dismiss this approach until you have tried it with all three stages. It does take time, and can't be rushed, so allow at least an hour.

Stage 1: Preparation

Take a notebook and write down these questions:
- How am I feeling?
- Where am I going to pray?
- For how long?
- With what passage of Scripture?
- What gift or grace am I asking God for?

Then write down your answers. They don't need to be long, and you don't need to think too much about them – just write down your initial thoughts. The first question might only need a one-word answer. Just take note of how you're feeling.

The next two questions make a conscious choice about the physical context in which your meditation is going to take place. Ideally, do the preparation and the review stages in a different physical space from the meditation itself. Even just changing your chair is helpful. Then consider how long you have to give to the next stage. Will you do the imaginative meditation for ten or thirty minutes? In a way, it doesn't matter how long you give it, but what is important is that you decide, write that time down now, and commit to it. At the next stage, if you don't feel you are getting anywhere, commit to keep going at it for whatever time you have decided in advance. Fifteen or twenty minutes is a good time to begin with.

On a retreat, your spiritual director will 'prescribe' certain passages for you as you work together, but at home don't worry about choosing the 'right' passage. I suggest you start with the story of Bartimaeus, given here. This approach works best with episodes from Jesus' life in the Gospel narratives. Choose a story in which something happens, in which Jesus interacts with people, rather than a parable or section of teaching. Try to use relatively short sections so that you don't have to worry about forgetting what happens! Now read the passage through two or three times so that you know it well and don't have to keep referring to it. It helps to copy it out by hand into your notebook at this point — taking the effort to write it out physically means you notice all the detail in the passage.

The last question might seem odd at first, but it was one of Ignatius' core insights that identifying and asking for a specific grace or spiritual gift really makes a difference. Sometimes you know exactly what you want to ask God for. It might not seem very holy or spiritual or achievable, but write down whatever comes to mind. Often there won't be anything in

particular, and that's OK too; there are various lists of gifts of
the Spirit in Christian tradition and in the Bible, so see if one
of these jumps out at you:

- From Isaiah 11:1–2: Wisdom; understanding; counsel;
  strength; knowledge; 'fear of the Lord' (often understood
  either as piety or a sense of awe).
- From Galatians 5:22–3: Love; joy; peace; forbearance/
  patience; kindness; goodness; faithfulness; gentleness;
  self-control.

If one of those resonates with you as something you particularly
wish for at the moment, write it down. If not, then just pick one.

Don't be tempted to answer these questions just in your
head; do write down your answers. This is important at the
review stage, when it is all too easy to forget what you thought
at the beginning.

Stage 2: Imaginative meditation

Now move to the place where you have decided to do this
central meditation. You've already chosen the passage to contemplate, and have read it through several times, perhaps written it out, so you can put your Bible and notebook down and
settle yourself comfortably. Close your eyes and begin building
the scene in your imagination. At this stage you're not working through the story, just setting the scene. I find it helps to
go through each of the five senses in turn, in this order:

- What can you see? Don't expect instantly to imagine the
  scene. Consciously construct it by asking yourself some
  questions about what you might expect to see given what
  you know of the passage. For example, is there a road?
  What kind of road? How many people are about? Are

you in a town or in the countryside? What's immediately in front of you? If you lift your gaze, what's in the distance? The scene might still feel sketchy, but that's OK.

- Now flesh it out some more by moving onto the next sense. What can you feel? What physical sensations can you imagine would be present – perhaps the heat of the sun? Move your toes – what does the ground feel like beneath your feet? Imagine moving your fingers or stretching out your arm – what textures can you touch?
- What can you smell, or what smells do you think would be around?
- Now imagine that the volume is turned up. What can you hear? What are the ambient sounds – birdsong? Animal noises? A confused babble of crowds? Market traders shouting their wares, perhaps, or is it calm enough to hear your own footsteps?
- Finally – a tricky one – taste. Are you eating or drinking anything? Or is your mouth dry in the heat? Can you taste the dust of the road, perhaps?

Going through each sense, let the scene build in your imagination. Don't worry about 'what really happened' or 'what it would really have looked like'; this isn't an exercise in biblical reconstruction, it's letting God work through your imaginative daydreaming based on this scene.

Now notice who you are and where you are in the scene. Are you Bartimaeus himself, or Jesus, or one of the disciples, or a random bystander? Sometimes you will find that you have taken on a character in the story, and sometimes that you remain yourself, in the scene. Either is fine.

And now, imagine the main events of the story taking place. Watch and listen to what happens. And then, at some point before the story finishes, make sure that you yourself speak with Jesus. If you've imagined yourself as one of the main characters this will have happened naturally, but if not then either go up to Jesus in your daydream-like imagining, or imagine Jesus turning to you. In this story, in particular, imagine Jesus asking you the question that he asks Bartimaeus: 'What do you want me to do for you?'. Answer him. Have a conversation with him. (If, as very occasionally happens, you find that you've imagined yourself as Jesus in the story, then try seeing what emerges if Bartimaeus turns round and asks you the question posed in the story.)

Sometimes it is hard to get Jesus to speak with you in the story, or you find yourself very much on the edge of the crowd and it all seems a bit distant. In that case, try speaking to whoever is standing next to you. What takes place if you turn to them and ask them a question about the scene you've both just been watching? And/or, what happens if you deliberately imagine making the decision to walk over to Jesus, and catch his arm, and tell him not to leave until you've spoken with him?

Stay with the story for most of the time you've decided, even if you don't seem to be getting anywhere. Or even if the story is finished and there is still time to go, don't leave; perhaps turn to someone else in the scene for another conversation, or even say to Jesus 'There's more time, what else?' Similarly, if you're only halfway through the story when the time is up (perhaps you've set a timer on your phone), feel free to leave at that point, trusting that God has given you what you need. You can always revisit the story on another occasion if you want to see what happens next. Then, when the time is up, draw whatever conversations you are having to a close and leave the scene. Finally, spend a minute or two mentally talking with God 'as one friend talks with another', as Ignatius put it, about what you have just imagined and experienced.

Finish with some definite gesture – perhaps make the sign of the cross, or say the Lord's prayer.

92

Stage 3: Review

Now get up and take a short break. Maybe make yourself a cup of tea. Taking your notebook again, write down these questions:

- How do you feel now?
- What happened?
- What moved you most? When did you feel the strongest emotional or even physical reaction?
- How or when did God feel most present or absent?
- What do you want to say to God now?

Write down your answers to these questions, one by one. The first tends to be quite short. As at the preparation stage, it's about noticing and being mindful of how you feel, without any judgement. Just observe how you are feeling and note it down briefly.

The second question is the one that requires the longest answer. Describe what happened in your imagination. What did you see, hear, smell, touch, taste? What happened when the story played out? What did Jesus say to you, and you say to Jesus? Don't worry if you can't remember everything, or if the sequence of events seems a bit muddled as often happens in dreams. Just note down and describe what you can remember.

Then there are two questions that are there to ensure you don't miss anything in this review. First, you are asked to identify the moment or moments when you felt most strongly moved – that is, when you felt the strongest emotional reaction. This could be a positive or a negative reaction. Did you feel suddenly furious, or a moment of intense loneliness, or jealousy, or envy? Or did you become aware of happiness, contentment, joy or peace, at some particular point? Did something that someone said, or did, spark a reaction in you that took you by surprise? Sometimes the answer to this question is obvious, but on other occasions it takes considerable thought to identify.

Next, ask yourself when or how God felt most present and/ or absent to you. Which was it? Or can you identify moments of both?

And finally, what do you want to say to God now? Write down your answer.

It is worth revisiting your notebook again, perhaps the next day or following week, and rereading what you have written. If you feel that there is unfinished business – perhaps you didn't get all the way through the story, or you are left feeling puzzled or unsatisfied by one particular part, or you want to ask something more – feel free to repeat the prayer exercise. Don't, though, try to replicate the whole experience again. Instead, go back to the part where you left off, or where something happened that you want to revisit, explore or change, and focus on just that section.

If you are using this material with a group, there are a couple of things to be aware of. First, make sure that you give people time to complete the exercise. If you choose to read out the initial, scene-setting questions (what you see, hear, feel, etc.) then make sure you give a good minute or two of silence for people's imaginations to work. There are few things more annoying than a guided meditation where the leader just keeps talking! When it comes to the main section (then what happens) leave what might seem like an uncomfortably long time of silence, perhaps ten minutes. Don't try to talk through the story in any detail, as people may well have gone off in all sorts of different directions in their heads, and find your questions distracting.

Second, ensure that people spend the time writing down their own review sections in silence, before discussing with others. And ensure that any discussion stays fairly general – don't expect people to share what might be very deeply personal insights with the group.

Try this with any episodes from the Gospels in which Jesus interacts with people, such as Mark 1:16–20, Mark 14:2–9 or Luke 19:1–10.

PART THREE
Molecular gastronomy: reason

15

Form and genre

Read: John 1:1–14

In the beginning was the Word, and the Word was with God, and the Word was God. He was in the beginning with God. All things came into being through him, and without him not one thing came into being. What has come into being in him was life, and the life was the light of all people. The light shines in the darkness, and the darkness did not overcome it.

There was a man sent from God, whose name was John. He came as a witness to testify to the light, so that all might believe through him. He himself was not the light, but he came to testify to the light. The true light, which enlightens everyone, was coming into the world.

He was in the world, and the world came into being through him; yet the world did not know him. He came to what was his own, and his own people did not accept him. But to all who received him, who believed in his name, he gave power to become children of God, who were born, not of blood or of the will of the flesh or of the will of man, but of God.

And the Word became flesh and lived among us, and we have seen his glory, the glory as of a father's only son, full of grace and truth.

Have you ever read a topical news story on social media and been outraged, only to discover that it wasn't genuine news, but came from a satirical website? We can easily recognise satire when it is packaged in a stand-up comedy programme, but it can take us unawares when we aren't expecting it. Genre, and being aware of what genre we're encountering, matters.

You can easily recognise a fairy tale, in English, because it starts 'Once upon a time'. Other languages and cultures have similar standard openings that signal the genre of the story that is to follow to their listeners. In Chile you are exhorted 'Listen to tell it, and tell it to teach it'. In the Yoruba language, from West Africa, stories begin with the joyful announcement 'Here is a story! Story it is.' 'In that only place' is how stories open in the Tamil tongue, while elsewhere in India, Teluga speakers begin their stories, 'Having been said and said and said ... ' In each case, the genre (a folk tale, a fairy story, etc.) is signalled by the traditional opening words. But if I were to hear that opening without knowing the linguistic traditions of the genre in a given language, I wouldn't necessarily know what to expect.

Form criticism arose out of a wave of interest in and study of folk tales and oral storytelling traditions in the nineteenth century. This was the time that the Brothers Grimm were compiling their famous collections of German folk tales. Linguists and historians were fascinated by what the study of oral traditions could reveal about the unwritten history of ordinary people in various times and places. It was also a time when archaeologists were unearthing large numbers of ancient texts in the Near East, from the ancient cultures that were Israel's neighbours and contemporaries such as Assyria, Babylon and Sumeria. Many of these newly discovered texts revealed startling similarities with the Hebrew Scriptures, raising the intriguing and unsettling possibility that the Old Testament was not as unique as had generally been assumed. And this wasn't a case of one or two similar stories arising in more than one place. There were law codes, origin myths, apocalyptic visions and collections of prophecies, proverbs or hymns that were all excitingly, or disturbingly, similar.

These two strands of study came together in form criticism, which initially aimed to reconstruct the oral tradition that lay behind the Old Testament. In doing so, form critics hoped to understand better the social and historical contexts in which these texts were composed, transmitted, told, retold and finally written down. At first, form criticism was confined to the study of the Old Testament. It rested on an understanding that the ancient Hebrew texts, particularly the Pentateuch, had gone through a long period of oral transmission before being committed to writing. The Hebrew script in which the Scriptures were written was one that omitted vowels: it seems to have been intended primarily as a memory aid for storytellers rather than as an authoritative text. And it was well known that rabbinic tradition included the retelling of stories with the addition of midrash (teaching or interpretation) that each teller would add as seemed appropriate for their own context. The ambitious project of form criticism, then, was to try to identify the form or genre of each section ('pericope', a unit), and by analysis of the norms, linguistic features and comparisons with other contemporary writings, try to identify what was the original oral tradition. The ultimate aim was to reconstruct the *Sitz im Leben* – the 'situation in life' or historical context – in which each element of the tradition arose.

Form criticism soon expanded its scope beyond the initial focus on reconstructing oral tradition. It became clear that literary forms were not as fixed and stable as had first been thought, and so instead of the form of a text determining its origin, it became appreciated that an understanding of genre was crucial to interpretation. It also became clear that the initial focus on individual pericopes, or small units of text, paid insufficient attention to the process of how these texts came to be put together into the books that we now read. Modern scholarship tends therefore to speak of 'genre' criticism instead of form criticism, and the study of the editing process has its own specialist name: 'redaction' criticism.

Form, genre and redaction criticism rely on considerable knowledge of ancient languages and linguistics. They also involve detailed comparison with other forms of ancient literature, changing as our understanding of these grows with each new discovery. Many of us will have heard, for example, that the Genesis accounts of creation and a great flood have significant similarities with other ancient Near Eastern creation myths, notably the Gilgamesh Epic. But it is much less widely known that even the ritual and legal elements of the Pentateuch have very close parallels in the literature of their ancient neighbours. For example, the whole structure of the book of Deuteronomy as a covenant between God and Israel is modelled on the form and content of contemporary neo-Assyrian treaties and loyalty oaths. Reading it in this light gives a fresh perspective on how Deuteronomy sets up a contrast between the people of Israel, who have God as their 'king', and other nations who are limited to treaties with human rulers.

It wasn't long before scholars began to apply the insights and methods of form criticism to the New Testament. Again, the aim was initially to investigate how the process of collecting together oral traditions about Jesus led to the Gospels. Just as with Old Testament studies, the initial focus on the oral transmission of stories soon widened to take in all sorts of other considerations of genre and style. Rudolf Bultmann, for example, a major figure in early-twentieth-century biblical studies, wrote a 1921 book *History of the Synoptic Tradition*, which is still influential today. Bultmann saw part of the task of form criticism as demythologising the Gospels to make them more acceptable to a twentieth-century audience, by clearing away what he saw as the confusing accretions of a first-century mythological worldview. This hampered the reception of some of the insights of form criticism among those who preferred to take the Gospel accounts literally. But an awareness of genre and the process that the New Testament books have gone through to take the form we read today can be enlightening whether or not you find demythologisation convincing or helpful. For example, Mark's Gospel makes frequent use of the Greek connective word 'kai': 'and then'. This gives the narrative a somewhat breathless immediacy and urgency, but form criticism adds the knowledge that 'kai' is a tell-tale marker of a rabbinic technique known as pearl-stringing, where stories, images or examples are picked from the tradition and strung together on a central thread or theme.

Perhaps the best-known and most widely accepted insight of form criticism is that certain passages, such as the Prologue to John's Gospel with which this chapter begins or the song of Christ's humility in Philippians 2:6–11, almost certainly pre-date the book that we read them in, preserving older early Christian traditions. These texts, identified by differences in grammar, language and form from the texts that now surround them, give us a glimpse into what the earliest Christians, even before the books of the New Testament were written, found central – and into what the Gospel and letter writers thought it was essential to pass on.

Ultimately, form criticism reminds us that the books of the Bible use a variety of different forms and genres, and are to some extent shaped by the norms and expectations of those genres. One of the fascinating things to realise is how the various authors didn't simply use the genres available to them, but at times subverted them (like those satirical news sites) or played with their readers' expectations to drive home their point. This is a way of reading the Bible that takes seriously the fact that the texts we read today have been through a long process of compilation, editing and adaptation, and that this was not accidental. The various writers and editors involved at each stage were, consciously or unconsciously, aware of the forms and genres that they used; the form they used is part of the message that they were conveying, and so is worth paying attention to.

This is not an easy approach to try at home, relying as it does on considerable knowledge of other sources and linguistic norms. But we can all ask the questions that genre criticism gives us, while online searches can supply a wealth of information very quickly. Try asking, for example:

- What genre is this particular passage? What does the fact that the author chose this genre add to my understanding of the text?
- If I consider the idea that this might be a different genre from the one that seems most obvious to me, how would that change my understanding of it? For example, what if this were a parable or myth, rather than a historical record? What if it were a letter or poem rather than a rule? How do I feel about those possibilities and why?
- What is the context, the form, of the whole book, letter or section that this passage occurs in? Has the way the material been arranged been chosen to draw out a particular point or suggest a particular comparison? Should this story be read in a compare-and-contrast way, for example, with something that immediately precedes or follows it? Can we tell anything about the history of the time, either the time this text was originally composed, or the time over which it was transmitted or preserved,

from the fact that *this* story was one that was chosen to be told and retold?

If you read Bible commentaries, try to notice when they are using this kind of information to help you understand the meaning of a passage.

16

Liberation theology

Read: Exodus 3:1–8a

> Moses was keeping the flock of his father-in-law Jethro, the priest of Midian; he led his flock beyond the wilderness, and came to Horeb, the mountain of God. There the angel of the LORD appeared to him in a flame of fire out of a bush; he looked, and the bush was blazing, yet it was not consumed. Then Moses said, 'I must turn aside and look at this great sight, and see why the bush is not burned up.' When the LORD saw that he had turned aside to see, God called to him out of the bush, 'Moses, Moses!' And he said, 'Here I am.' Then he said, 'Come no closer! Remove the sandals from your feet, for the place on which you are standing is holy ground.' He said further, 'I am the God of your father, the God of Abraham, the God of Isaac, and the God of Jacob.' And Moses hid his face, for he was afraid to look at God.
>
> Then the LORD said, 'I have observed the misery of my people who are in Egypt; I have heard their cry on account of their taskmasters. Indeed, I know their sufferings, and I have come down to deliver them.

Liberation theology developed in the Americas in the 1960s, born of the Civil Rights Movement and the base communities of Latin America. Key thinkers such as Gustavo Gutiérrez (whose 1971 book *A Theology of Liberation* gave the movement its name) and Leonardo Boff meant it has come to be particularly associated with Roman Catholic thought.

The Latin American context of the time included a toxic combination of serious and increasing poverty, political oppression and violence (protesters routinely 'disappeared', murdered by political regimes which would not tolerate dissent) and increasing injustice in areas such as land ownership. In the United States, the Civil Rights Movement similarly arose out of the racism, violence, lynchings, economic and political marginalisation that were (and still are) the continuing long-term results of slavery. Church leaders, like so many other community leaders, were involved in protesting against these injustices but were sometimes also complicit in them, as they navigated their own survival. This context was foundational to the development of liberation theology, which arose from a passionate conviction that God cares about the plight of those who are being oppressed.

If the gospel is good news, it must be good news for the poor, marginalised and oppressed, not just for the ruling elite. Yet too often in the Christian past (particularly in the context of the history of Spanish and Portuguese colonisation of Latin America and in the history of slavery) theology and biblical interpretation had been used to tell the poor that they should bow to their oppressors. The idea of salvation had become so spiritualised that almost any level of oppression or brutality could be treated as theologically irrelevant, since salvation was about achieving life after death, not about the conditions of life here and now. Liberation theology was consciously revolutionary, insisting that the Latin American context should be allowed to shape and change traditions of theological doctrine and biblical interpretation; that what happened now, politically and economically, was as important to theology as life hereafter.

There are four main strands to liberation theology that shape a liberationist scheme for reading the Bible. First, it took a bottom-up approach, emphasising the importance of reading the Bible from within your own context. In Latin America, this particularly took the form of small groups of Christians known as 'basic ecclesial communities', or 'base communities', often lay led and meeting in homes, reading the Bible for themselves and rejecting church traditions of an authoritative interpretation. This strand is covered more in chapter 17, on the hermeneutics of suspicion.

Second, it is about seeing theology, or reading Scripture, from the perspective of the poor, the oppressed and the marginalised. God's Word is seen as being spoken to us not just in Scripture, but in the life stories of the poor all around us, and in the ways in which history has shown us cycles of oppression and liberation. Within Scripture itself, this approach asks us to identify not with the rich, powerful or influential characters in a story but with the poor, marginalised, humble or excluded. This has become relatively mainstream in sermons and commentaries in recent years, so it can be hard to remember how radical it once was to read a story from these 'non-heroic' perspectives. So, for example, the story of Exodus was traditionally read as the story of Moses, the great hero. Liberation theology asks us to read it from the perspective of the outcast and oppressed, as the story of liberation of a people who are enslaved and exploited. So, most obviously, the extract given above makes it clear that God has not only *heard* the cries of the oppressed but *cares* about them and, moreover, *intends to act* to change their situation. Notice too that Moses himself, at this point in the story, is an outcast, a criminal on the run. He is described as being literally in the wilderness when God meets with him in the burning bush, a dramatic symbol of God's startling intimacy with people at the margins of society. Furthermore, reading this story now, with our developing awareness of genocide and oppression as something other than just the history of winning written by the victors, our attention also tends to be caught by that long list of peoples who already make their home in the land flowing with milk and honey. How does this story read from the perspective of the Canaanites, Hittites, Amorites, Perizzites, Hivites and Jebusites?

Third, liberation theology redefines the classic metanarrative of fall and salvation (which is discussed fully in chapter 21). For liberation theology, salvation *means* liberation. This is a major shift from the approach common from the early medieval period, which focused on the Genesis story of creation and the fall as an interpretative framework for the whole Bible. In that metanarrative, humanity's big sin that Christ came to reverse was seen as disobedience to God's command not to eat the fruit of the tree of the knowledge of good and evil. Christ's obedience to death on the cross reversed or recapitulated that initial act of disobedience and thus brought about salvation. It is easy to see how this version of events, however spiritually uplifting, could be extremely useful to the ruling powers. Indeed, many of the early documents of the English Reformation are quite startling to modern eyes in their confident assertion that being a good obedient subject to the Crown is the way to salvation for normal members of the public. Slavery, empire and widespread oppression were all justified on this basis. For liberation theology, the big sin of humanity that Christ's saving death reverses is not disobedience, but greed. Humanity's temptation to greed lies at the root of oppression, injustice and violence, as we seek to ensure that we have access to more than our fair share of the world's goods. The salvation offered by Christ is liberation from this sin of greed, which is not just a matter of bad individual moral choices but is structurally embedded in our social, political and economic systems. On this reading, 'freedom in the promised land' is not simply a metaphor for heaven, but a manifesto for radical change now.

Fourth, and finally, liberation theology is more concerned with doing the right thing (orthopraxis) than holding the right beliefs (orthodoxy). This isn't to say that doctrine is unimportant, but that the key test of whether beliefs are, in fact, right is whether they lead to right (i.e. liberating) actions. If doctrines are experienced as oppressive by the poor, they are likely to be incorrect and need revision.

In practice, then, a liberation reading starts from the assumption that the overarching story of Scripture is one of liberation. The test of whether any given interpretation is authentic is whether it tends towards liberation rather than oppression. If a given interpretation is experienced as oppressive by the poor, but liberating by the privileged members of a society, it is likely to be wrong. Conversely, if it is experienced as liberating by those who are marginalised, but oppressive by those who are privileged, it is likely to be right. This is known as 'the preferential option for the poor'.

This means that it is hard, if not impossible, to do liberation theology from a privileged perspective. If you're reading this, as I'm writing it, in a relatively privileged position, then, whatever you do, don't simply pretend that you are reading it 'as if' you were poor. Liberation theology is all about reading Scripture, and doing theology, in and from your own context, not wondering 'What would the poor think of this?'. Instead, seek out and be informed by what the poor themselves have said. To do this for yourself, you need to identify where (if) you are oppressed, and read from that perspective, ideally with others. Liberation theology is at heart a group exercise.

We have all become increasingly aware of the complexity of privilege in recent years and the extent to which different aspects of privilege and/or oppression intersect in each of our bodies and lives. This concept of intersectionality means, for example, that I have white privilege at the same time as experiencing a certain level of oppression as a woman living in a society that is still formed by patriarchy (see chapter 18 on feminist interpretation). 'White privilege' does not imply that I necessarily feel, or even am, particularly privileged; it simply means that the colour of my skin is not something that disadvantages me in the society in which I live. In recent decades, liberation theology has informed and sparked many different strands of interpretation, each authentically using their own different lenses and perspectives. Black theologies, womanist theologies, feminist theologies and queer theologies are all parts of this liberation theology family. In the following two chapters, we'll consider first a key underlying technique that is important to the practice of liberating interpretation – a hermeneutic of suspicion– and then, because it is one that I can authentically speak to from my own perspective, we'll consider feminist interpretation as an example of these identity-based liberation theologies.

17

A hermeneutic of suspicion

The hermeneutic of suspicion is the first interpretative approach that we've looked at that did not originate in biblical studies. So we're going to begin this section not with a reading from the Bible, but with a very different exercise – an exercise in seeing what isn't there.

Take a piece of paper and a pen or pencil and sit where you can see a chair. A traditional, wooden four-legged chair is best for this exercise but use what you have, perhaps a desk chair or a table. Now do a quick sketch but don't draw the chair. Instead, I want you to draw the spaces where the chair *isn't*. What shapes do the gaps form?

* * *

When we sit down to draw a chair, it's hard to get the perspective right. Our brains tell us that we know what a chair looks like: it has a seat, a back, and four legs. It's almost impossible to see the true angles in front of you because your interpretation of what we should be seeing gets in the way. This is the insight behind this way of reading the Bible. We have to do our utmost not to see in it only what all our religious and cultural assumptions tell us must be there. We have to make a conscious effort not to focus on the words that are there (the chair) but on what has been left out. Drawing in the gaps will make the chair itself come into fresh perspective when we stand back and look again.

Hermeneutics or the study of interpretation is not limited to studying the Bible but applies to all texts. And 'text', here, doesn't just mean the written word; it means anything that you are interpreting. So in media studies, a 'text' might include a film or an advertisement. In archaeology, it might be a building, or the faint marks on a field scan showing where human activity once took place. Pictures, objects and any sort of media are all 'texts' that we interpret.

You may have come across, for example, the recent fashion for histories of a topic 'in a hundred objects' where artefacts are examined for what they can tell us about social, economic and cultural trends. For the purposes of reading the Bible, this means that our understanding of what the 'text' is can be expanded beyond the words that are written on the page to include the physical presentation and packaging of those words. Issues like whether the different books of the Bible were published individually or together; the size and presentation of the book as an object; and the ways in which it has been produced and disseminated (from being hand copied in monasteries and convents to being the bestselling printed book of all time), all influence our interpretation of what 'the Bible' is and means, and how it has been handled (both literally and metaphorically) through history.

The hermeneutic of suspicion focuses on something even further removed from the simple study of the words on the page; it encourages us to ask about, and listen to, what isn't there —to see the gaps or listen to the silences.

The phrase originates in the writings of the twentieth-century philosopher Paul Ricoeur who was particularly interested in the philosophy of interpretation. Ricoeur coined the phrase 'the masters of suspicion' not in biblical study, but to describe Karl Marx, Friedrich Nietzsche and Sigmund Freud.

He was describing an underlying similarity in their very different approaches to seeking meaning in texts. Each of them assumed that texts tell us something beyond what their authors intend. They were each suspicious of what texts purported to be about, arguing that what their author, and their readers generally, would say they were really about was not their most important, or even their 'true', meaning.

For Marx, the real interest and meaning of any text lay in what it says about the means of production. It might be a Bible, a novel or a newspaper, but whose labour lies behind it? Who is making money out of it – and who is not? Freud's suspicion was focused differently. He was looking for the sublimated sexual urges that the author of any text would insist it was not about, but which he suspected drove much creative effort and literary argument. For Nietzsche, the real meaning would be found in looking for the unstated power relationships that underlie a text's production, dissemination and interpretation, as well as its argument or content.

These challenges have been indirectly taken into the heart of modern biblical scholarship, particularly in the development of the range of approaches known as liberation theologies. In biblical studies, a hermeneutic of suspicion involves looking at the text and asking a series of questions, suspiciously interrogating the text and our received understanding about it. These might be questions arising out of the insights of Marx, Freud or Nietzsche, but might also arise from any other lens of suspicion that we choose to use.

The process is rather like using different coloured filters over a camera lens to show up particular contrasts better or to emphasise a certain lightwave length. The key insight of a hermeneutic of suspicion is that there is no such thing as a 'no filter' reading of the Bible. Normally that filter is whatever is culturally privileged in our own society and worldview. We all have a series of cultural assumptions that we tend to think of as 'just common sense'; unless we deliberately choose to swap out that filter for others, we may never even notice that it *is* a filter. That is how privileged worldviews get perpetuated – we don't even realise that they are privileged because they seem to be just the way things are. So, for example, black theology, feminist theology, womanist theology and queer theology all look at the text with a particular filter, seeking to isolate and explore particular aspects of the text that may have been over-looked or de-emphasised by a history of interpretation that has marginalised those perspectives.

It is true to say that when using this technique you will see what you go looking for to some extent. But that doesn't mean it is wrong – it is a feature, not a bug. If you put a par-ticular filter over a camera lens you will enhance certain wave-lengths in what you see but you're not creating colours that weren't there in the first place. It's also crucial to recognise that you're not, so to speak, putting on blue, yellow or pink filters when what you had before was plain glass; you're simply swapping out your existing coloured lenses for a different one. There is no such thing as a plain glass view and if you believe you're reading Scripture without any filter you are deluding yourself. This is what it means to 'check your privilege' in this context: to pause and recognise that there is inevitably a filter of cultural assumptions that you bring to your interpretation of any text.

So when you interact with a text, be suspicious of what you read and, in particular, be suspicious of uncritically accepting what 'everyone says' the passage means. The general principle can be summed up in two key questions: 1. Who or what is missing from this story? 2. Whose interests is this serving?

To take an example: a Marxist analysis uses the filter of asking about labour, the means of production, and economic and class relations. When you look specifically for these in the text, what comes to light? So, for instance, a story about a feast might not mention the labour of those who have cooked, prepared, set up the tables and will clean up afterwards. Where is the money coming from to pay for all these things? Does telling the story as a story of the elite, where servants are just assumed, help perpetuate a system where elites are taken for granted as the important players, the named characters; and does this lead to or perpetuate an assumption that the elite are the ones in whom God is most interested or the ones who are most religious, and perhaps most valuable? Or further, where do you see God in the story? Do you assume, or have you always been taught, that God is the equivalent of the rich landowner, the king, or the lord in the passage? How does it change your reading if you interpret it as a story in which the behaviour of the elite man is critiqued, in which God is represented by another character with less economic, political and social capital? You might also ask questions about the economic system in which the physical artefact of the Bible has been produced.

To take another example, feminist and queer theologies have a particular interest in looking for instances where characters don't conform to expected gender roles or stereotypes, and in focusing on those characters and their stories. Queer theology has developed the feminist interest in gender binaries into a broader concern with the existence and 'queering' of all kinds of binaries. So much of popular culture, now and in the past, uses the shorthand of looking at the world in terms of binary pairings – male/female, gay/straight, black/white, Jew/Gentile, in/out, clean/dirty, good/bad, rich/poor ... the list goes on. Queer theology applies a filter that specifically looks for what binaries are represented in the text, and/or in traditional readings of the text, and examines whether they are used in a way that reinforces or challenges ('queers') that binary way of thinking. Similarly, queer, feminist, black, womanist and other liberation theologies will all ask questions looking with their particular filter at what is missing, and whose interests are being served. Questions you might ask include:

- Who isn't in the story who should be? Whose voice is not being heard?
- How would the story look if it was told from their perspective?
- In whose interests was it to include this story in the canon of Scripture?
- How have you heard this story typically interpreted? Whose interests does that interpretation serve?
- What are the power relationships going on in this story?
- What are the gender relationships going on in this story? Are typical gender roles enacted or challenged?
- What are the class or economic relationships? Where is the economic power?
- Where's the sexual power in the story? Who wields it? Whose fantasies are fulfilled or challenged?
- What are the political arrangements or assumptions? Are they challenged or reinforced?

In the following chapter, we'll look in more detail at feminist hermeneutics, as a case study in this kind of approach.

18

Feminist interpretation

Read: Exodus 1:15–19, 2:1-10

The king of Egypt said to the Hebrew midwives, one of whom was named Shiphrah and the other Puah, 'When you act as midwives to the Hebrew women, and see them on the birth-stool, if it is a boy, kill him; but if it is a girl, she shall live.' But the midwives feared God; they did not do as the king of Egypt commanded them, but they let the boys live. So the king of Egypt summoned the midwives and said to them, 'Why have you done this, and allowed the boys to live?' The midwives said to Pharaoh, 'Because the Hebrew women are not like the Egyptian women; for they are vigorous and give birth before the midwife comes to them' ...

Now a man from the house of Levi went and married a Levite woman. The woman conceived and bore a son; and when she saw that he was a fine baby, she hid him for three months. When she could hide him no longer she got a papyrus basket for him, and plastered it with bitumen and pitch; she put the child in it and placed it among the reeds on the bank of the river. His sister stood at a distance, to see what would happen to him.

The daughter of Pharaoh came down to bathe at the river, while her attendants walked beside the river. She saw the basket among the reeds and sent her maid to bring it.

When she opened it, she saw the child. He was crying, and she took pity on him. 'This must be one of the Hebrews' children,' she said. Then his sister said to Pharaoh's daughter, 'Shall I go and get you a nurse from the Hebrew women to nurse the child for you?' Pharaoh's daughter said to her, 'Yes.' So the girl went and called the child's mother. Pharaoh's daughter said to her, 'Take this child and nurse it for me, and I will give you your wages.' So the woman took the child and nursed it. When the child grew up, she brought him to Pharaoh's daughter, and she took him as her son. She named him Moses, 'because', she said, 'I drew him out of the water.'

Feminist readings of Scripture include a hermeneutic of suspicion (see the previous chapter) which, as we've seen, asks in whose interests a given text was written, and even whether (and if so, how) a text so bound up in patriarchy in both its authorship and traditions can be of any value to women. The American academic and theologian Mary Daly was a leading exponent of this line of questioning. Feminist interpretation also includes an interest in gender binaries and their subversion, which has been developed more fully in queer theology. This present chapter will explore three other key areas that are fundamental to feminist biblical interpretation. First, there is a focus on noticing and paying attention to the women's stories that are in the text, but which have been marginalised or ignored by traditional readings. Second, feminist interpretation seeks to raise our consciousness of the underlying narratives about, and typical portrayals of, gender roles, that a text perpetuates, subverts or explores. And third, feminist interpretation pays particular attention to issues of the gendered use of language and imagery, together with its implications for our reading of Scripture and the theology we derive from it.

Elisabeth Schüssler Fiorenza, one of the most influential early feminist scholars, was among the first to draw attention to ways in which women's stories in the Bible, and in early church history, have been overlooked and marginalised. Fiorenza called her book *In Memory of Her*, a quotation from Matthew's Gospel. Matthew 26:6–13 recounts the story of a woman pouring a jar of expensive perfume over Jesus, while the disciples complain of the waste of money that this represented. In response, Jesus first justifies her action by speaking of his forthcoming death, and then says this: 'Truly I tell you, wherever this gospel is preached throughout the world, what she has done will also be told, in memory of her' (Matthew 26:13, NIV). It's the only place recorded in the Gospels where Jesus explicitly says that a particular story, and a particular person, must be remembered alongside him. Yet it would feature very low, if at all, on most people's lists of key Gospel passages. First, then, feminist interpretation pays attention to the often overlooked stories of women that are hiding in plain sight in our texts.

The passage from Exodus with which this chapter begins is a good example. The story of the baby in the bulrushes is well known as the story of Moses' birth, centring him as a great hero in the tradition of epic narratives. In Christian theology, parallels are often drawn with the baptism of Jesus – the central saviour figure coming out of the water with a new destiny. Yet read afresh, with an eye to looking for women's stories, this is a story about women. Almost all the main characters are women, and their experience and agency are what drives the action.

The two midwives, Shiphrah and Puah, are rare examples of women who are named in the text in their own right, a dignity not afforded either to Moses' mother or to Pharaoh's daughter in this story. They are the key heroic figures in this story. Their courage in resisting Pharoah's destructive and cruel order begins the Exodus narrative of liberation. I love the fact that they use the intimate nature of their 'women's work', and male squeamishness about it, in their defence. They are marginalised as low-status women, but they are able to use what power they have (their knowledge of childbirth processes and Pharoah's ignorance of them) to achieve their desired ends with impunity. They even adopt the trope that low-status women are more 'animalistic', more vigorous in childbirth — a racist assumption that even now means black women are offered less pain relief in childbirth than white women — in their favour. Their rhetoric uses Pharaoh's own prejudices against him. Shiphrah and Puah are not simply minor characters whose actions incidentally allow Moses to survive so that he can become the liberating hero; they themselves begin the work of liberation, starting a cascade of female empowerment.

Moses' mother, her baby spared by their actions, is empowered to hide him for three months and then, when he is presumably getting too big and noisy to hide anymore, attempts her basket-rescue mission. We may wonder whether the princess' unnamed attendants, themselves enslaved Hebrew women, might have been willing accomplices in this rescue. Was the whole thing planned in advance by this group of women between themselves?

The princess, who despite her privilege probably had little political or economic power of her own, is able to utilise what privilege she has. She does not seem to have been concerned that her desire to adopt the child might be rejected or forbidden. The princess, like the midwives, uses men's assumptions about women, and prejudices about status, in her favour. Adopting a baby plays into widespread cultural assumptions about the naturalness of women's maternal instincts, and the maternal desires of high-status women have often been satisfied by taking children from those lower down the social scale. She seems to have rightly assumed that her desire to adopt this child would be indulged.

Finally, Moses' sister (named later in the story as Miriam, an important prophetess in her own right) is both watchful and bold. She is the one who most models not just what might be considered 'natural' maternal love or womanly compassion but strategic thinking, tactical timing and bold action. Miriam monitors the situation, and then identifies exactly the right moment to act. In a breathtaking stroke of audacity, she deftly engineers a situation whereby their own mother is paid for nursing the child through infancy.

All the main characters in this story are women, and it is they who save Moses, not the other way round. There is no male hero riding to the rescue of a princess here; instead, the princess comes to the rescue of the helpless male infant. So this story is also an example of the feminist interest in narrative structure and the ways in which texts form or subvert gender norms. This aspect of feminist interpretation draws on form and genre criticism (see chapter 15) and links with a wider interest in women's studies in narratives, stories and roles. From a biblical studies point of view, one of the most interesting aspects of this is that the biblical stories so frequently undermine or subvert expected gender roles or narrative arcs.

This story of Moses in the bulrushes subverts the key patriarchal narrative that women are helpless without a male rescuer. Read this way, the opening of Exodus is a story that demonstrates just how effective women's agency and determination can be in the face of oppression and male violence. It shows that women can work together even on both sides of a political, ethnic or class divide to subvert the roles that have been drawn for them and bring liberation. It shows that women can subvert the harmful assumptions of male privilege (that it is natural for an elite woman to desire a child, and acceptable to use slave labour to achieve this end, for instance; or that it is natural for lower-status women to be more 'animalistic' in their birthing habits) to achieve their own ends. It shows women claiming and owning their enjoyment of traditional nurturing roles while fulfilling roles as active architects of their own fate.

So feminist interpretation is about noticing and looking afresh at women's stories, which are there in the text but often ignored by traditional readings. Feminist interpretation asks us to look again at the women in the Bible and see them not just as supporting characters to the male heroes, but as leading ladies in their own right.

Another aspect of seeking out women's stories is to notice when they are not simply overlooked in the tradition, but are actively hidden from us by the language chosen. So, for example, in Mark's, Luke's and John's accounts of Jesus feeding the five thousand, we are told that there were five thousand men present. Matthew's version of the same events is alone in noting that there were five thousand men – besides women and children. The women and children literally do not count. Or to take another example: we are familiar with the historic English usage of the male pronoun to include the female – 'men' being used to mean 'people' – but perhaps not so alert to the fact that the original languages that are being translated have similar linguistic conventions that privilege the male. Typically, a male collective noun was used to describe any mixed-sex or all-male gathering; a single man present would mean the male noun was used. In other words, women are under-represented in the text when they may not have been under-represented in the historical events described. On other occasions, biblical translators have been so sure, given their assumptions about gender roles, that a woman cannot be intended by the text

121

that they have insisted that a female name must be a male one (for intance, Prisca or Junia in Paul's references to early church leaders).

A related linguistic example can be found in the words used for God. We are very accustomed to thinking of God as male, by analogy with patriarchal imagery of king, lord and father. Some of this bias is indeed original, but a significant proportion of it is imported into the text by linguistic convention. Have you ever noticed that sometimes, in the Bible, the word 'LORD' is capitalised? That capitalisation denotes that the word being translated is not the usual human word for lordship, but the Hebrew 'tetragrammaton': the four letters YHWH which stand for the name 'God' revealed in Exodus 3:1–8 (see page 104) – 'I AM WHO I AM'. In rabbinic tradition, this word was not generally spoken aloud, and instead the reader would substitute an alternative such as 'God' (Hebrew *elohim*), 'the Name' or 'Lord'. In some English translations, it is common practice to honour this tradition by writing not 'YHWH' but 'the LORD'. This practice, though, gives many a reader the impression that God is almost always referred to by a word that is essentially masculine – the exact opposite of the revelation in Exodus of God as essentially nameless, Being itself. Try replacing every occurrence of the capitalised LORD with I AM whenever you read the Bible and see how different it feels.

When you are reading the Bible, then, notice the women who are there, either those who are named as key actors in the text or those whose likely presence you can infer. Which women are not named – where is the invisible labour of women, for example? It's worth specifically seeking out the stories of women, as many Bible reading plans and church lectionaries under-represent their often troubling stories. Investigate, for example, the stories of Hagar, Judith, Jael or Tamar – stories that are rarely heard in church. In whose interests might it be to focus on other stories, of women whose gender performance is more in keeping with societal norms? How do their stories challenge prevailing patriarchal narratives or expected gender roles? As a general principle of feminist interpretation notice the women; name them; and let their stories be heard as women's stories, not simply as the background to a male narrative.

19

Ecology

Read: Mark 4:3−8

> 'Listen! A sower went out to sow. And as he sowed, some seed
> fell on the path, and the birds came and ate it up. Other seed
> fell on rocky ground, where it did not have much soil, and it
> sprang up quickly, since it had no depth of soil. And when the
> sun rose, it was scorched; and since it had no root, it withered
> away. Other seed fell among thorns, and the thorns grew up
> and choked it, and it yielded no grain. Other seed fell into
> good soil and brought forth grain, growing up and increasing
> and yielding thirty and sixty and a hundredfold.'

One of the most interesting new directions in biblical scholarship is an ecological reading of Scripture. By this I don't just
mean looking at the stories through an environmental lens or
asking what they teach us about our relationship with the earth
– though that comes into it – but using our new scientific and
old lived understandings of ecosystems and their interactions
to look afresh at the biblical narrative.

Ecology is more than simple biology. As a science, it's about
not just looking at individual plants and animals but paying
attention to their interactions with other organisms and with
their wider environment. A weed, for example, might be
revealed to be an essential part of an ecosystem. Perhaps that

weed flowers at a time when nothing else does, and so is critical to the survival of bees and other pollinating insects, without which other plants that are critical to the food chain are
unable to reproduce. Lacking those other plants, small insects
and rodents are unable to survive and the food chain is dis-
rupted.

The Bible uses a lot of organic imagery. Vines and vine-
yards are recurrent images for Israel and for God's work on
earth, while trees are often images for the growth of kingdoms, dynasties or nations. Perhaps one of the most instantly
recognisable biblical images is of the garden of Eden, with Eve
picking and eating the fruit from the tree of the knowledge of
good and evil. Throughout the Bible, humans interact with
their environment. They struggle to grow food and worry
about the provision of water; they battle wild animals and tend
domesticated ones; they use natural resources to build struc-
tures and cities, and cope – with varying degrees of success –
with natural disasters, weather and climate phenomena.

An ecological reading of Scripture invites us to take this
organic imagery with the utmost seriousness, and to consider
it holistically. Most traditional readings of scriptural organic
images focus on reading them either allegorically, or as simple
illustrations. But what happens if, instead of focusing just on
the plant, animal or organic process described, we consider
them in the context of a whole ecosystem?

In the parable of the sower, a farmer is interacting with
their environment by sowing seed. The parable describes
different elements of the physical environment that the
farmer is interacting with. There are various types of soil and
ground conditions – some have been compacted as a path
by human activity; some are naturally rocky with only a thin
covering of soil; and there are also fertile and productive
areas. There are weather and climate considerations, most
notably, the hot sun. Then there are other living organisms

besides the human farmer that interact with the seed – birds that eat it and brambles that out-compete it for nutrients in some places.

Typically, readings of this parable focus simply on the human subject, the farmer, and on the item that they are dealing with – the seed. Even the seed is seen only in relation to its utility to the human subject, who desires a harvest for their own subsistence and profit. This is an example of an 'anthropocentric' reading – one that puts humans (from the Greek word 'anthropos') at the centre of how we see the world. Other organisms and environmental factors are seen as relevant only to the extent that they help or frustrate the human endeavour at the centre of the story. The tone was of course set for such readings by the interpretation of the parable given in Mark 4:13–20. From analysing the original language and speech patterns used, scholars agree that this is almost certainly a later interpretation by the early church, at the time the Gospel was being set down on paper. The interpretation sees the farmer in this story as an evangelist who is sowing 'the word' of the good news about Jesus, and the various soils as the people who are receiving it. It was probably written at a time when the early church was struggling to understand why their message, if it was indeed from God, was encountering so much opposition – a good example of how we can (perfectly legitimately) read the stories that Jesus told in the light of our own particular concerns and contexts.

You may well find such an anthropocentric reading spiritually helpful and informative. But when you come across a story like this, which has such a rich collection of environmental and biological factors in play, try an ecological reading of such passages as well.

Ecologists think in terms of five layers or levels of increasing complexity. Individual organisms; populations; communities; ecosystems; and, finally, biosphere. At each of these levels there might be both biological and non-biological factors (such as the sun and the rocks in the parable) that come into play.

1. Organisms are individual living things (a bird, a seed, a bramble plant, etc.). Ecological studies of individual organisms consider behaviours and adaptations as the organism interacts with and adapts to its environment.
2. Several of a single organism become a population, so we might talk about the population of birds in a particular area or the population of brambles. Ecological questions to ask about populations include their size, density, structure and how they change over time.
3. The combination of all the populations in a particular area is a community, in which different populations interact with one another − birds eating seeds and berries or humans planting seeds, for example. At this level, the focus is on the interactions between different populations, and how those interactions shape and are shaped by the community and the physical environment.
4. An ecosystem is made up of the community in an area along with the non-biological factors (sun, rocks, soil type, availability of water) that affect and influence that community. Ecological studies of ecosystems often focus on the recycling and circulation of nutrients.
5. Finally, the biosphere is the globe, the planet Earth, and ecologists working at this level look at the interactions between different ecosystems and global patterns, such as climate and the movement and distribution of species.

At each level ecology looks for emergent properties, things that are greater than the sum of their parts because they arise (emerge) not from the individual components themselves but from their interactions.

We can use this structure as a guide to noticing and considering the organic imagery in the story holistically. First, what are the individual organisms involved? Notice each one – in our case, human, seed, birds, brambles. It sounds obvious, but we are conditioned to focus on the human subject and the objects they particularly interact with. The first step in an ecological reading is not to give greater weight to the human subject and what is useful to them in the story. Rather, notice and name each individual organism as of equal value.

Second, look for populations. In this story, there are two: 'the birds' and 'the thorns'. We don't know the size of these populations, but we do hear something about the density and development of the population of thorns – they grow up, thickly enough to out-compete for nutrients those seeds that have taken root in the bramble patch. Third, consider the community that is described here: how do the various populations interact with one another? For example, in this story notice that those seeds that take root in the bramble patch do grow (they're not entirely killed by the brambles) but they don't receive sufficient nourishment to set seed. The brambles are better at taking up the available nutrients, perhaps, or maybe just limit the seeds' access to sunlight. The birds have at least two potential sources of food: the seeds that the farmer sows and no doubt berries from the brambles later in the season. The brambles in the story are in their spring growth phase, though, so the farmer's seed is currently the only other source of food mentioned for the birds, unless there are other plants growing in the area. We don't know if there are, but a farmer may well have cleared and weeded the field in order to sow the seed, quite probably in the process removing plants that otherwise would have fed the birds at this time of year.

What about the whole ecosystem, with this community of birds, seed, brambles and humans interacting within a physical environment? It sounds like fairly marginal land, hard to farm, with its rocks and hot sun. I wonder if the concentration of rocks in certain areas has been caused by human activity over time, moving scattered rocks and stones to the margins of the field, to make the ground easier to cultivate. Human activity has also clearly made a path, where either soil has been compacted by frequent traffic or perhaps stones have been deliberately placed to form a boundary path. So human activity over time has altered the environment in which the birds and the brambles and the seed interact, creating areas where the seed will take root more easily, but also contributing to the fact that the seed can't flourish in other places.

And what of the seed and seedlings themselves? They are so easily thought of as simply inert objects handled by the human agent in this story, but they too interact with their environment, and in ecological terms they are nutrient-rich. Let's take a moment to consider the story of the seeds themselves, in terms of the cycle of nutrients within an ecosystem. Some of the seeds are eaten by birds, providing them with nutrition at a time of year when it may well have been hard to find. That nutrition will in turn return to the earth eventually, in the birds' guano and later in their corpses. The seeds that grow up and wither in the shallow soil will probably remain where they lie. Over time, they will contribute to the deepening of that shallow soil layer over the rocky ground, and eventually that soil will provide a home for other plants – seeded here by the birds – which will flourish in such conditions. And next year the seeds that grow thinly among the brambles will provide a layer of compost-mulch for the bramble roots. Maybe that grassy-straw layer, which will remain when the brambles die back, will provide more winter cover for insects and small mammals, who will add further complexity to the ecosystem.

In an anthropocentric reading, the seeds that don't grow to harvest are wasted, while those that do flourish are valued numerically according to how fruitful they are for the human agent. From an ecological perspective, though, nothing is wasted. In traditional readings of this parable, seeing it as a parable for mission and evangelism, the assumption is that the seed that doesn't fall on fertile ground, and so does not produce its harvest – thirty or sixty or a hundredfold – is wasted effort. But on an ecological reading, even the seed that doesn't produce the desired harvest has an important part to play in the ecology of the whole system. How does this perspective change the impact of this story on you?

You might want to go even further and consider this story, or others, on the global, biosphere level. You could ask, for example, how this ecosystem might interact with others, locally, regionally or globally. If this story were a microcosm of human interaction with our planet, what might it be telling us?

Try reading any passage of Scripture that makes use of organic imagery in this way. Pay attention to each of the five ecological levels and particularly look out for and consider interactions between different factors and the complexities that emerge at each successive level. Perhaps spend a moment retelling this story from the perspective of the non-human organisms. How would this story go if it were being told by a bird? Or a seed? Or a bramble?

20

Experimental play

Read: Luke 6:46–9

'Why do you call me "Lord, Lord", and do not do what I tell you? I will show you what someone is like who comes to me, hears my words, and acts on them. That one is like a man building a house, who dug deeply and laid the foundation on rock; when a flood arose, the river burst against that house but could not shake it, because it had been well built. But the one who hears and does not act is like a man who built a house on the ground without a foundation. When the river burst against it, immediately it fell, and great was the ruin of that house.'

Modern computer games rarely have instruction manuals. Games now are designed to be immersive learning environments, where you find out what to do by exploring a world and the available tools and resources for yourself. Increasingly, companies and education software providers are exploring how to 'gamify' other ways of learning. This isn't to trivialise them, but to take seriously the fact that we often learn better by doing than by being told things.

Church, faith and reading the Bible are often presented as rather intellectual exercises. Theology is something that some people learn and then teach to others, trying to ensure that they get it right. In other words, we can easily slip into treating

Christianity as primarily an educational experience, like school. We can then find that we begin to think of it as something we either succeed or fail at.

Various approaches to church and Bible reading have explored this theme in recent years. Often, they have arisen out of a desire to make the faith more accessible to children and young people. Or they have been developed by people who wanted to put into practice in the life of their church what they had learned from educational theory about learning styles and experiential learning practices. For example, Godly Play was developed by Rebecca Nye and Jerome Berryman inspired by Montessori theories of education and learning. In a Godly Play session a Bible story is translated into a simple 'acting out' with neutral figures and natural materials, followed by an extended time for undirected artistic and creative responses. One of the fastest growing forms of church over the last couple of decades has been Messy Church, in which an extended period of creative engagement with a focal Bible story is combined with a short worship session and then a sociable meal. Founded by Lucy Moore, Messy Church has since grown to a loose network of over 3,700 congregations registered with the Messy Church organisation, in thirty or more countries. Many more churches and congregations, while not officially affiliated, have been influenced by the Messy aesthetic and principles. Other emerging expressions of church, such as Forest Church and Sweaty Church, have built on this approach, focusing more specifically on engaging with the natural environment or through physical games and exercises. You can read more about Messy Church and Godly Play on their websites (www.messychurch.org.uk and www.godlyplay.uk).

Sadly, however, the fact that these and other creative approaches have been associated almost exclusively with children's spirituality means that they have tended to be sidelined as an alternative to 'real', grown up church. Messy Church is clear that it is meant to be all-age and is emphatically not intended to be a children's craft club, but nevertheless it is frequently dismissed as primary-school focused and so marginal to the important work of developing adult and youth discipleship. In my experience, though, the creative engagement with the biblical texts that these approaches encourage is valuable for adults of all ages and abilities, as well as for children and young people.

What has emerged, through these and other initiatives in recent decades, is a distinctive, creative approach to reading the Bible – what I call a 'hands-on hermeneutic'. A hands-on hermeneutic encourages you to enter into a scriptural passage in all sorts of physical and creative ways. As you do so, you explore the emotions, context and questions that the story evokes. You don't read the passage as an intellectual exercise, asking what it means and how it applies to you; instead, you let your body and your creative response surprise you with the insights they give you into the reading.

This is a way of reading the Bible that, by its very nature, does require some equipment. This can be as simple as a piece of paper and a pencil, but your experience will be richer if you have a much wider variety of art materials and other objects and activities to hand. For that reason, this approach, more than any other in this book, works best as a group exercise. It also benefits from some advance preparation. I'll outline first how to prepare for a group session, and then give two much simpler ways of trying this, either alone or with others, with minimal preparation or supplies.

As an example, we'll take the well-known story of the man building the house with and without good foundations (in other translations, built on rock or sand) with which this chapter began.

Creative exploration of the passage as a group: a sample session outline

If you have time to plan and a space to prepare, then try setting this up as a series of 'stations' – different tables or areas for people to move around, each with a single activity exploring one aspect of your theme or passage. Depending on the size of your group and the time and resources available, I would aim for between five and eight stations or activities and allow about an hour. Make it clear that people can go around the activities in whatever order they wish, and engage with each one for however long they wish – they haven't got to get round everything. You can either have a person stationed at each table to run the activity, or simply have written instructions and/or a reflection at each point. It may help to explain briefly each activity at the beginning before encouraging people to explore for themselves.

The team planning the activities will find that meeting to think through the reading in advance, and planning what activities to use to explore it, is a remarkable Bible study activity in its own right. You will need to think about what activities to plan that will draw out reflection on different aspects of the reading. Try to be imaginative in planning activities that will engage a range of different senses and ways of thinking or acting: drawing, physical play, building, exploring textures, using smell and so on. There are books and magazines available that give sample crafts and activities for a range of Bible readings, such as the Messy Church materials, but avoid thinking of this as simply delivering a pre-planned session. And remember that the activities, crafts and games are not ends in themselves! A major danger in delivering this sort of session is to slip into thinking of it in terms of producing 'good' end results – a display for the wall, something to show and tell. The point of the activities is always to enter into the story, not to produce polished artwork. If you think this could be an issue for your group, then plan activities that don't have a finished product but are all about the experience.

For example, if I were running a session exploring this story, I might have the following stations set up on tables around the room:

1. Exploring building on sand, comprising a sand tray and a collection of beach pebbles. How many can you balance?

2. Exploring building with and without firm foundations, presenting a collection of Lego® bricks, with base plates and also with a selection of alternative base materials (carpet samples, bubble wrap, compost, turf or gravel in a tray).

3. A game of Jenga (either the normal table-top version or, if someone has it, the large, garden version) for people to play, to help you enter into the real sense of frustration when something collapses!

4. A prayer station to encourage reflection on what the foundations of your life are. Perhaps this could take the form of a cairn. People spend some time contemplating what is important to them and then add stones to a cairn, either silently naming each stone with what is important or writing on them.

5. Building with inappropriate materials – how high a construction can you make using just marshmallows and dried spaghetti?

6. What words of Jesus do you find it easy to put into practice? And which ones do you find much harder? You could have two flipcharts or sections of wall and a supply of sticky notes for people to add their thoughts to throughout the session and read what others have put.

7. Finally, I'd normally include a colouring and drawing table, with a good selection of drawing materials and

both plain paper and a colouring sheet based on the story. There are innumerable free printable colouring sheets for most Bible passages to be found online or you could simply get someone to write out a part of the passage in 'bubble' writing for people to colour in, and photocopy enough copies of that for everyone.

At the end of the session, gather everyone together (or split into small groups, depending on numbers) and discuss what emerged from the session for you. Perhaps bring the cairn into the centre of the circle and spend some time praying for good foundations.

A simpler group version

A simpler version that I've found very effective in both mixed-age and all-adult groups is to divide people into tables, café-style, and on each table put a box of Lego®. It doesn't matter what selection of bricks each group has – they don't all need to be the same. Do try to include a good selection of figures in each box, though, preferably with a variety of different facial expressions.

Read the reading and give each table a copy. Then ask them to model the story or an aspect of the story. Make it clear that they are free to work individually or in one or more smaller groups as they prefer. Give them a time limit – say ten minutes – and a one- or two-minute-to-go time call.

Then go round each group and ask them to show their models, explaining which aspect of the story they have chosen and why. You'll be amazed at the different details of the story that various people have picked out, and at the depth that you will all have considered the story by the end.

Just pencil and paper

Finally, the simplest low-tech, no-prep approach is simply to give each person paper and a pen or pencil before reading the passage. Explain that you're going to read the story and you want them to illustrate it or draw whatever comes to mind as it is read. Make it clear that this is not an art competition! Stick figures, cartoon strips and doodles are all fine.

Explain that you will read the story twice and then leave a bit of time for people to complete their drawing. Ask everyone to put the tip of their pen or pencil to the page, and then start reading. At the end, invite everyone to share what they have drawn and talk about it. During the Covid-19 lockdowns, this is what we did with one of our church small groups, meeting online. Everyone – adults and children alike – drew or sketched during the Bible passage or story, and then we all shared our pictures via a messaging group while we discussed them live online. If you're on your own, try simply sketching or drawing in response to the Bible passage. Some people do this directly on the page of a journalling Bible.

This approach can work well with most parts of the Bible but is easiest with passages where there are clearly sensory elements to explore. Parables and stories from the Gospels work well, but try it also, for example, with Ezekiel 37:1–14, 1 Kings 19:3–13, or Acts 2:1–21. This is also a good way to explore the Christmas or Easter stories, whether with families, schools or adult groups.

21

Dramatic theology: performance and improvisation

Read: Hebrews 1 (abridged here to 1:1–5, 10–12, NIV)

In the past God spoke to our ancestors through the prophets at many times and in various ways, but in these last days he has spoken to us by his Son, whom he appointed heir of all things, and through whom he made the universe. The Son is the radiance of God's glory and the exact representation of his being, sustaining all things by his powerful word. After he had provided purification for sins, he sat down at the right hand of the Majesty in heaven. So he became as much superior to the angels as the name he has inherited is superior to theirs.

For to which of the angels did God ever say:
    God: 'You are my Son;
    today I have become your Father'?

Or again:

    God: 'I will be his Father,
    and he will be my Son'?

He also says:

> *Narrator:*'In the beginning, Lord, you laid the foundations of the earth,
> and the heavens are the work of your hands.
> They will perish, but you remain;
> they will all wear out like a garment.
> You will roll them up like a robe;
> like a garment they will be changed.
> But you remain the same,
> and your years will never end.'

The words in italics are my own addition, but they simply emphasise the playscript nature of this passage. This whole chapter is made up of a series of quotations (or near-quotations), mainly from the psalms. Some are in the first person, God the Father speaking, and some in the second person, speaking about God. But more than that, this chapter summarises the dramatic sweep of a 'big story' reading of Scripture, what is known as a metanarrative. All of history is seen as part of God's big drama being played out on the world stage.

Hebrews presents the story of salvation as a drama in four, or maybe more, acts. Act 1: Creation. Act 2: Israel's story, in the Old Testament, featuring the prophets. Act 3: The dramatic entrance of Jesus, an unexpected yet brilliantly satisfying plot twist. Act 4: Jesus is in heaven sitting at the right hand of the Father ... and we wait to see what happens next. Maybe this is the last act, maybe there is a lot more to come. We are given a teaser, that things are going to change dramatically over time – like a series of costume changes – but also (spoiler alert) the reassurance that there will be a happy ending. We can enjoy and throw ourselves into the rest of the story, because we don't need to worry about God being dethroned in a last-minute upset.

The main characters are clearly the two figures of God the Father and the Son. But there are all sorts of other characters whose role in the script is hinted at: prophets, our ancestors, us, angels. This is a huge production, with a cast of countless millions, and only the whole of creation is a big enough stage for its performance.

This way of thinking about the Bible has developed since the 1970s, first as narrative theology (with an emphasis on reading the Bible as a big story) and more recently as dramatic theology (with an emphasis on us being participants in the ongoing drama). Dramatic theology is particularly associated with the theologian Hans Urs von Balthasar, who wrote four volumes under the title *Theo-Drama: Theological Dramatic Theory* in the 1980s and 1990s, but it has become widely recognised and used. It is one of the contemporary approaches to reading the Bible that has been broadly embraced by many in the evangelical movement, who appreciate its dual emphasis on taking the story of Scripture seriously, and on the practical acting-out of our faith in the world. But it is also embraced by catholic and progressive theologians from a wide variety of perspectives.

Dramatic theology sees the Bible as 'the Script' of a big story. The details differ between different theologians, but there are many common features. The main character, the protagonist, is God – either simply God, God the Father or Jesus. In von Balthasar's Trinitarian scheme, the Father is the author, the Son is the main actor and the Holy Spirit is director of the action. The main drama is the interaction between God and humanity. The story is seen as taking place in several acts, though different theologians differ over the precise details of how many.

Narrative theology, the forerunner to dramatic theology, proposes that this is the big story, the metanarrative, and that we find meaning for our own lives within this bigger picture.

Dramatic theology says this isn't just a story that's told and that we reflect on – it's an ongoing drama that we find ourselves caught up in. We're not just watching the drama unfold as an audience, we ourselves become the actors making the script come alive and improvising how it's going to develop. Baptism, if you like, is our moment of being dragged up on stage in front of our cheering (or perhaps jeering) family and friends, for our moment of audience participation to begin. We are the actors in the current act of the play. On this understanding of what it is to be a Christian, discipleship is about being formed in the script and traditions of performance so that you can faithfully play your part in a collective, ongoing endeavour in 'putting on Christ' in our own time and place.

Some proponents of dramatic theology describe our task primarily as performance, faithfully delivering the script. Others focus on the improvisational nature of this drama. These lead to rather different ways of understanding Scripture as the Script. A performance view sees the Bible as the definitive author's script for us to learn and then enact. But this is not to say that we simply 'read the script'. A dramatic performance is very different from a reading of a script. On this understanding, the Bible is only fully itself when we embody it and enact it. The analogy is with a Shakespeare play, which is only fully what the author intended when it is produced on a stage, with real flesh-and-blood actors and audience, not when it is an object of academic study by Shakespeare scholars. The script (the words on the page) are important but they need actors (us) to bring them to life.

Improvisation, on the other hand, is by definition unscripted. Improvisation in the theatre doesn't mean just making things up as you go along; it requires practice and highly developed skills of attention to your fellow actors. There's an art to keeping the dialogue going and making it believable and interesting. If you've ever had a go at improvisational theatre, or seen others do so, you'll know that it is all too easy to shut down the conversation or figuratively paint yourselves into a corner. It's important that your focus is on the other actors in the scene, not on the audience and how they may be responding. It's important, too, that your focus is on listening to and observing what those other actors are doing, so that your own actions and words are in response to them and can build on them creatively. So, for example, it is helpful to make choices and suggestions that open up other possibilities, rather than close them down, and to respond to other actors' suggestions positively and in a way that keeps the conversation open – 'Yes, and … ' rather than 'No, this'. And so theatre exercises for improvisation tend to focus on developing three main areas: observation, listening and team building. There are obvious analogies here with the way in which we read the Bible as a church rather than just as individuals.

Since improvisation has no script, the Bible clearly can't be the script in this understanding. Instead, it is seen more as a record of the improvisation that took place in the previous acts which set the scene for our current improvisation and give some clues as to what future acts will hold. There are limits, therefore, on what we can freely improvise; it might be different from what has gone before but it needs to be authentically responding to and arising from it. Similarly, we don't know exactly where we're going, but what we do with the story needs to make it possible for those who come after us to move in a plausible direction. Some might describe the Bible as a jazz musician might describe a record: the recording of a moment in time, of an inspired performance by some of the greats of the past, giving themes and melodies for us to learn, practise with and ultimately improvise around ourselves. Contemporary theologians such as Sam Wells argue that improvisation is a good model for Christian ethics. We can't know what new ethical situations will arise in the future, and many won't be covered in 'the Script', so we can't simply perform what we read in the Bible. But if we know it well, and have allowed ourselves to be formed by it, both individually and as communities, we can trust that our improvisation will be faithful.

Performance and improvisation, though, are not as opposed as they might initially seem. Those who think in terms of 'performing the script' recognise that there is always an element of improvisation in how we 'put on Christ' in any given situation; while those who focus on improvisation assume a deep familiarity with the material that has gone before, which will shape our creativity.

If you are reading this book as a group, you could try spending one of your sessions working on a series of theatre exercises – there may well be someone in your community who could lead these, or there are examples that can be found on the internet (search 'improvisation drama games'). Spend most of your session time on these exercises, before moving to focus on a biblical passage. Read the passage two or three times, and then in pairs or small groups try various exercises exploring the text through drama. For example, you could simply try acting it out, but with simple limits (only two people, only one minute, or you must incorporate a random object allocated to each group – a chair, a hat, a balloon, etc). Or in groups of, say, four or five people, you could plan and create, using only your own bodies, a still tableau expressing the passage. Give yourselves ten minutes to plan what you are going to do, then present it to the rest of the group. When everyone has performed, discuss the differences and similarities between your offerings, and why you each made the choices you did.

But you don't need a group of people to do drama exercises with in order to read Scripture in this way. You can simply read a passage and reflect on it as a scene in the great drama. Which act do you think it fits into? In terms of the overall theme of God's interaction with humanity, what is this scene doing to advance the story? What would the play be missing without it? Does it develop character, build up tension or reveal a surprising plot twist? If you were going to dramatise this for television, who would you cast in the main roles? Where would you set the action? What camera shots would you plan?

Afterword

by *Paula Gooder*

The image of reading Scripture as eating bread is rich and evocative and, as Miranda points out in her Introduction, reminds us powerfully of how nourishing Scripture can be. I, too, have been sustained and nourished on my journey of faith through my reading and reflecting on so many parts of the Bible. The image of the Bible as bread brings to mind the word 'companion'. Although we no longer use it like this, the word 'companion' comes from the words 'with' (*com*) and 'bread' (*panis*). So a companion is someone who breaks bread with you. In this sense, the Bible is a perfect companion. It accompanies us on our journey through life, providing support and nourishment whenever we need it.

The Bible itself is a worthy companion on the way, but the word 'companion' also reminds us of one of the key features of reading the Bible that has come through so strongly in this book. The Bible is better read in community, with others, with companions. As we seek to read the Bible, one of the most important things that we can do is to seek out companions, those who will break bread with us, as we seek to read and to be nourished by the word of life. Sometimes companions can help us to understand what we are reading on those occasions when a passage feels beyond us. One of my favourite examples of this is the story of the Ethiopian eunuch in Acts 8:26–40. When Philip first saw him, the eunuch was reading a bit of Isaiah and was asked by Philip 'Do you understand what you are reading?' He replied 'How can I, unless someone guides me?'. We must surely all have had a moment like that when reading the Bible, when we simply have no idea what it means and feel in need of someone to help us make sense of it.

Companions – a broad community of readers – can also help us hear different voices or perspectives on what we are reading. A brilliant example of this comes from the work of Mark Allen Powell. He read the story of the prodigal son with three different groups – one from America, one from Russia and one from Tanzania. He asked each one why the prodigal son ended up so poor: the Americans said that it was because he had wasted all his money, it was his own fault; the Russians said it was because there was a famine in the land, there was nothing he could have done about it; the Tanzanians said that it was because no one in the new country offered him hospitality and looked after him. The thing is that all three groups were right. All three answers are in the story but the culture and experiences of each group shaped what they saw. This reminds us of the importance of making sure we 'break bread', the bread of Scripture, with as many different companions as possible, from as wide a range of cultures and experiences as possible. If we limit the companions we read the Bible with, then we risk (to extend the metaphor a little) eating just white sliced bread while others are feasting on focaccia and naan bread.

There is just one problem with the image of reading the Bible being like eating bread – it makes it sound easy. You find the bread, you pick it up and eat it. Job done. You will be aware at the end of this book, though you probably knew it already, that reading the Bible is far from easy. It takes time and care; it requires thoughtfulness and dedication; it isn't always easy but it is worth it. So persevere with your reading, even when it feels that you are gnawing on a dry crust rather than savouring a delicious loaf, fresh from the oven.

Sometimes reading the Bible can feel dispiriting and hard, but in my experience it is worth continuing; the long-term nourishment is well worth the effort and, when times are hard as they have been lately, we will need all the strength we can muster to carry on.

Appendix 1: A note on Bible translations

If you've ever been in a group of people who have each read the same passage out loud from their own Bibles, you'll have immediately noticed the sheer variety of ways in which different editions translate the same words. People often ask, in some bewilderment, why there are so many different Bible translations and how they should choose the right or best one to read. Adding to the confusion is the fact that Bible translations are normally known simply by their initial letters (KJV, NIV, ESV, NRSV and so on) which can feel like a secret code.

So here I'll summarise some of the main points to be aware of in choosing a Bible translation and explain what the most commonly encountered versions are called.

Why so many?

Translation is not simply a matter of putting different words into an equation. It's not a mechanical process, like changing the colour of text in a document on your computer. Translation is an art, not a science. It involves making a series of choices, at both ends of the process. Choices have to be made about what the original words mean or meant and what modern words best convey that meaning to a contemporary readership.

Words in any language rarely have a single, simple meaning – they usually have a range of references and inferences. Think of a simple word in our language, such as 'stone'. It can mean the substance of rock – anything from gravel to a granite kitchen worktop. It can mean a small pebble or a huge monolith. It can be a unit of weight. It can metaphorically refer to hardness, or suggest that someone or something is unyielding or uncaring. It can refer to a method of capital punishment, or to a state of intoxication. Often the meaning will be clear from the context, but not always. Imagine a reader thousands of years from now, speaking another language and having learned English from only a very few surviving texts, trying to work out what 'he was stony faced' or 'she was stoned' meant in the early 2000s.

Bible translators often refer to an axis between dynamic equivalence and formal or literal equivalence. The Bible Society website helpfully describes these as 'thought-for-thought' or 'word-for-word' approaches respectively. In other words, are the translators more concerned with trying to find words that have the same impact on a modern reader as they would have had on an original reader, or with a strictly literal translation of the words themselves? So, in the example above, a dynamic translation might render 'stony faced' in a local equivalent phrase for that facial expression, whereas a formal translation would use the local words for 'stone-like' and 'face'. In a dynamic translation, a 'stone' in weight would be converted into the equivalent units that the reader would be familiar with, whereas a formal translation would tell us that the original unit was called a stone.

The proliferation of different Bible translations are, therefore, a result of different individuals – or, more often, committees – making a series of different choices about where on this equivalence axis they want to be. Different versions are also the result of developing scholarship shedding new light on what the original languages might have meant; of stylistic choices relating to the constantly changing way in which contemporary language is used and understood; and of theological considerations, which inevitably influence which of a range of possible translations are considered viable.

A simple guide to some common Bible versions

Most of the 'code' of those TLA (Three Letter Acronym) titles can be fairly easily interpreted when you know what the most common letters stand for. 'V' stands for Version and 'B' for Bible. 'E' refers to English (usually meaning that this version uses British English spellings and idioms rather than American English). Because translations are often updated as language and scholarship change, 'N' for New is also quite a common prefix.

At the time of writing some of the best-known translations are:

- The New International Version (NIV) – the current best-selling version, the NIV aims to strike a balance between literal translation and conveying the meaning clearly to a modern audience. Considered somewhat conservative theologically, but widely used.

- The King James Version (KJV) – also known as the Authorised Version (AV), the KJV is the original, official English translation dating back to 1611. It aimed to be an accurate translation, in beautiful poetic language (often archaic even at the time). Well-loved language and turns of phrase make this a perennial favourite for many, but it can be hard to read and, as language has changed, misleading in places. It was, of course, based only on the Greek and Hebrew texts that were available in 1611, so new translations are more technically accurate.

- The New Revised Standard Version (NRSV) – a contemporary version which is at the formal rather than dynamic end of the spectrum. It is favoured for accuracy of translation, (though this can make it less suitable for reading aloud and less poetic) and reliably uses inclusive language for humanity, except where the original text is clearly intended to refer to only one gender. The NRSV is widely used for study rather than for its literary quality.

- The New Living Translation (NLT) – a very colloquial translation, with the emphasis on conveying meaning rather than formal accuracy. Many people speak highly of this version's accessibility, readability and touch of poetry.
- The English Standard Version (ESV) – a consciously evangelical translation, at the formal end of the translation spectrum.
- *The Message* – a very colloquial translation, more of a paraphrase in places, using modern American idioms. *The Message* captures something of how fresh many of the texts would have sounded to an original hearer. Best read alongside a more straightforward translation.
- The Common English Version (CEV) – developed out of research into how English is read and understood, and designed for maximum accessibility for those who are not familiar with Bible jargon and traditional phrasing. Its commitment to inclusive language goes as far as translating 'Son of Man' as 'Human One', whereas most inclusive translations limit themselves to using inclusive language for humanity. The CEV has been awarded the Crystal Mark from the Plain English Campaign.
- The Good News Bible (GNB) – perhaps best known for its inclusion of line drawing illustrations, this is a very colloquial translation, designed to prioritise accessibility and readability. It is theologically quite conservative, and is considered rather dated now, but the drawings in particular have a certain nostalgic charm for many.
- The Jerusalem/New Jerusalem Bible (NJB) – the translation favoured by the Roman Catholic Church, the Jerusalem Bible translations include all seventy-three books of the Catholic Canon (including those books that the Protestant tradition refers to as Apocrypha). They are on the dynamic end of the translation spectrum,

favouring an often very beautiful poetic style. The NJB revision incorporates inclusive language.

The best version is several versions

The perfect Bible translation does not exist. That's why there are so many: not because everyone before has got it wrong, but because there is such a wide range of legitimate choices to be made in the art of translation. So don't waste time trying to find the perfect translation that will answer all your questions and resolve all the difficulties in the text. A good version of the Bible is the one that you have in front of you – and the best version is to have more than one.

Overall, if you are looking to buy a Bible for the first time, or to buy an additional version, then I would recommend you consider the NRSV, NIV and CEV. I also strongly suggest that, if funds permit, you spend your budget on buying two or three different cheap editions rather than one smart leather bound one. If possible, keep one that you don't mind scribbling in, and add notes, thoughts and doodles directly onto the text as you read, pray and think. As well as being a helpful way of remembering your thoughts, this encourages you to think of your Bible as a working document. You might even consider buying one from the increasing ranges of journalling Bibles, which have wide margins specifically designed for notes, doodles or the astonishing array of Bible study art that has developed in recent years. Search 'Bible journalling' online for inspiration if this is an idea that attracts you.

Having access to several different versions, so that you can compare them when you are studying a passage, is so much easier now in the age of the internet. There are several Bible websites and apps (such as www.biblegateway.com) that allow you to search for a passage and then compare translations. The internet also makes it relatively easy to look at the original languages, by using online 'interlinear' translations, which give you the original Greek or Hebrew text, with the literal rendering of each word in English underneath. An internet search for 'interlinear Bible' will find various options; you don't need to have any knowledge of the original languages to see what lies behind the various translation decisions that have been made. They aren't an everyday tool for most of us but can be fascinating to look at occasionally.

Try to get into the habit of cheerfully and intentionally reading more than one version – not to try to work out 'the right' translation, but to deepen your awareness of the complexities of the text.

Appendix 2: Using this book in a group

This book can be used as the basis of a church Bible study group or Lent course. It would work well to use the three sections of the book to form a sequence of three seven- to eight-week courses over a year. In 'Term 1' the material in the Introduction would form the first week of an eight-week course, followed by two seven-week courses. You could begin the year either in September or in January: these have been found to be the most effective start dates for introductory church courses, as both have a 'new start' feeling to them. You could also simply pick a few different chapters to form a course of whatever length fits your group.

Suggested running order for sessions

Begin session 1 with introductions. The best way I've seen this done is to ask everyone to say what their name is and to share a story that is associated with their name. This makes names so much easier to remember and works well as an ice-breaker exercise too. Never assume that everyone knows who everyone is! Asking people to share a story about their name is a good way to get those people who might otherwise say 'Oh, everyone knows who I am' to share their name. In the first session, you might also ask everyone to share briefly one memorable experience of reading the Bible.

In subsequent sessions, begin by going round the group asking people to speak for up to a minute or two about how they feel now about last week's session, or their experience of reading the Bible in the last week. To prevent some people speaking for too long, it can work well to use a jokey but very obvious timer – a big sand timer, perhaps, or a prominent kitchen timer. This also adds a gameshow element to this aspect of sharing which can stop it feeling too intimidating.

You may then wish to light a candle in the centre of the group and use an opening prayer. I would put this here, rather than immediately at the beginning of the session, to allow for late arrivals and to mark turning from a focus on the participants to a focus on the Bible. Use this, or another prayer of your choice:

> We light this candle as a sign of God's presence with us.
>
> God of light and love,
> give us, we pray,
> the grace and gifts that are your will for us today.
>
> Help us to hear and understand your holy word;
> to be aware of our own reactions and emotions;
> to be sensitive to one another's stories,
> and receptive to one another's insights.
>
> May our study of your word lead us into ever deeper
> gratitude for all your gifts,
> awareness of the communion of saints,
> and relationship with your Word, Jesus Christ.
> Amen.

Now you have various options for the main session input:
Either 1. Simply read out the content of the chapter that is your focus for this session. You could share this between several different voices, or even ask each person to read a paragraph in turn if everyone has their own copy of the book (and is confident reading aloud).

Or 2. Having read it yourself in advance, summarise it or say something similar in your own words, adapting it to your group as appropriate. You might ask different people from your church to do this in different weeks.

Or 3. You might run your session more like a book group, and expect people to have read the chapter in advance of each session. In this case you'll be able to have more substantial discussion, but if people routinely do not do the advance reading it can be disruptive for the group. If you take this option, then you might ask one or two people in advance to prepare a few minutes' introductory material sharing their thoughts on this approach, and then chair a general discussion. You might want to ask people not simply to read the material but to try it out in the week.

After the main input, I suggest that you leave a period of silence (two to three minutes), during which people are encouraged to consider what they have heard. Invite participants to be attentive during this time both to their emotional reactions and their intellectual questions. Encourage people to notice their own body – how are they feeling physically? What does this tell them? Encourage them to have a notebook and to note down in this time of silence any words, images, questions or whatever else comes to mind.

Now go around the group asking members to share one (or at most two) things that they have noted. Explain that these are to be received in silence, not discussed at this point.

Next, I would ask people to have a go at the particular approach to Bible reading that is the focus of the session. The way in which you do this will vary depending on the technique outlined in the chapter and the people you have in your group. You might, for example, choose a Bible passage in advance and ask two or three people to read it out, and then split into small groups to ask the questions or follow the approach of the chapter, before reconvening to discuss it. Alternatively, you might specify the passage and then simply ask people to go off and find some space to contemplate it on their own, using the framework or approach outlined, and then reconvene for a general discussion. You might prefer to stop your session at this point and set this as an exercise to be done in people's own time during the week, to be discussed at the start of the following session.

Finally, move to a period of general discussion and feedback as a whole group. Split this time into two, discussing both the passage that you were reading and the method of reading. These don't always have to go in the same order: let the group's feedback and energy determine on each occasion which goes first and how the time is divided between them.

You may wish to end with a time of open prayer or simply by saying the Grace together ('The grace of our Lord Jesus Christ, and the love of God, and the fellowship of the Holy Spirit, be with us all evermore, Amen').

Some notes on running a course online

I've trialled this material in an online course run on the Zoom video-conferencing platform, with around twenty participants. An online course works in a very similar way to an physical group, but I've found that there are some small changes that work better for the online format, and some different considerations to be taken into account.

The recruitment of participants, and therefore the type of people who join, may well be different if you run a course online. You can advertise an online course in various ways: create it as an event on social media, advertise it on your website and other online places, and perhaps ticket it on Eventbrite or a similar platform (which is free if you make the tickets free). Any of these methods enable your congregation, family, friends and social media acquaintances to share the link easily (do encourage them to do so!) and this can mean that people you have had no previous contact with might join you, from all over the country (or indeed overseas). Do be aware of this – it's a great missional opportunity, but you need to be prepared to be joined by people who may have very different levels of knowledge of the Bible or of Christian faith and very diverse life experiences. Remember that people who have joined by simply seeing the link online might not be thinking in terms of joining a local church group; they may have seen the link at third or fourth hand, and just be thinking of it as on online course on an interesting topic. If so, be careful to treat them as equal participants, and avoid in-jokes and letting discussions of the local church or area predominate.

Consider accessibility issues and take advice on these. Some of the issues differ widely from when meeting in person. For example, participants with hearing loss won't need a hearing loop, but could you offer a sign language translator or use a captioning option? Obviously, building issues such as steps and toilets won't be a problem, but what about the timing and length of your sessions? Some people will be using desktop computers, others tablets or smartphones, so think about the visibility of screenshared material on different hardware, and don't assume that everyone can see, say, all twelve participants at once on their screen.

My experience is that, although people often worry that online relationships aren't going to be as good as 'the real thing', they will get to know each other very well indeed over the course. Meeting online seems to create a particular intimacy among scattered participants, perhaps because they are each meeting from their home ground, and/or because they are used to using the online space for personal discussion and self-revelation in social media contexts. There is also a very real benefit in that people are labelled with their name, which is hugely helpful for those of us who are not good at learning names and don't want to offend someone by asking when we've seen them around in church for years! Do ensure that you ask people to label themselves online with their real names (whatever variant they want to be known as); sometimes people enter a meeting with a default label such as 'Dad's ipad', or are using someone else's account or device, and that can be somewhat disorientating for participants. If they don't know how to rename themselves you can do that yourself as meeting host: just ask their permission to do so and ask what name they would like you to use. Similarly, people can use the name field to specify their pronouns if they wish to do so.

The timing and dynamics of gathering are rather different. In a physical meeting, there is often a substantial period of time over which people arrive, during which we'd make a hot drink and catch up with how people are. Online, people tend to arrive promptly, and there is less appetite and scope for general chat. So while for a physical meeting I'd open the church or meeting room half-an-hour before the advertised starting time, an online meeting room only needs to be opened five minutes in advance. Again, in a physical meeting, I would often begin with some general greetings and some worship – a song, some simple liturgy. This functions partly to set the mood and partly to allow for late arrivals! Online, however, we found it worked best to greet people, and then get straight down to business, with simply a short opening prayer. Similarly, I might include substantial periods of silence in a group meeting in a church, but communal silence, though it can be powerful, does not work in the same way in an online group. Nor does singing or congregational responses.

Facilitating discussion requires some thought and infrastructure to work well online. Whole group discussion can be intimidating with a sea of faces all looking directly at you.

You can't simply ask people to turn to their neighbour and discuss something for a moment as it is not possible to have simultaneous conversations in the main group, and it is harder for people to sense when it is their turn to speak. For substantial discussion, it is best to have a version of your conferencing software that allows you to put participants into smaller breakout groups. You might then ask someone to feedback from each group. You can either plan who is going to go into particular groups in advance or allow the software to allocate people randomly – and if you do the latter, you still have the option to move people between groups when you see the groupings. Consider placing somebody in each group who you have asked in advance to take on the role of chair or facilitator. Practically, it is advisable to have a co-host for the meeting who is organising the breakout groups while you are leading the first part of the session.

Don't forget that the chat facility is also useful for doing discussion slightly differently. Using the chat, people can add comments or questions as they occur to them, and then they can be discussed at a later point. Some people are much more comfortable formulating a comment in writing, so it is helpful to offer both ways of engaging. Again, it might be wise to nominate somebody whose job it is to monitor the chat and identify questions, themes or topics to be discussed.

And remember to build comfort breaks into an online session, just as you would if meeting in person, and encourage people to get themselves a drink at that point.

Finally, I'd encourage you to think of some of the things that are different about online meetings as features, not bugs. For instance, some people dislike the fact that participants can turn off their cameras, or drop in and out, but it is worth noting that for some these are major advantages. Autistic people, for example, have repeatedly told me over this past year how freeing they find not having to participate in discussion – they can simply leave the room at any point without drawing attention to themselves. Others find not having to be seen extremely reassuring. And people for whom entering an unknown building and being confronted with an unknown group of people is a major barrier to trying church are finding online groups and worship a safe way to dip a toe in the water. Online, people are always free to turn off their camera and/or mute themselves, or simply unobtrusively leave, as they wish. This puts them in control in a new and liberating way. Online, we have entered into their space and are a guest in their home, rather than the other way round. Another feature that is very different from physical courses is the ability for participants to have simultaneous conversations, alongside or even totally ignoring whatever you have planned and are delivering as group leader(s). In a physical meeting this would often be considered rude or disruptive, but online it is normal etiquette for people to give simultaneous comment or have additional conversations. Try not to be put off but embrace it as a democratising feature of online meetings.

Appendix 3: Some suggestions for further reading

This is by no means an exhaustive bibliography, but a personal list of suggestions of books that I have enjoyed and think you would enjoy reading next. I have avoided giving a long list of academic references to authors and books that I have referred to in passing in this book, as some are in books or articles that are hard to find outside university libraries, while others are easily found by a simple online search. Many of the historic works referred to in this book are available as open access PDFs online.

The books mentioned here are ones that I have used myself with church study groups, so I can personally recommend them as books that are accessible to a wide and varied group, and all (apart from those more technical books mentioned at the end) would be suitable if you have read this book as a group and are looking for your next group book.

A good place to start if you are unfamiliar with the Bible as a whole is Sam Wells *The Heart of It All: The Bible's Big Picture* (Canterbury Press, 2019). This is a very readable example of understanding the Bible as a single overarching narrative or drama.

Paula Gooder has written widely on the Bible, and I'd particularly recommend starting with her *Phoebe: A Story* (Hodder & Stoughton, 2019) which is a semi-fictional imagining of what it was like to be among the first Christians receiving one of Paul's letters. The second part of the book explains the research behind key elements of the story. I loved reading this, and found it brilliantly evoked the variety of ways in which even the earliest Christians used and understood the New Testament as it was being composed. Try also her *The Parables* (Canterbury Press, 2020) for a good example of how to read these stories afresh.

If you would like to read more from me, then you may enjoy my short and very accessible introduction to the history of the churches, giving a wider context for how the Bible has been used and interpreted across the past two thousand years: *The Essential History of Christianity* (SPCK, 2012). I'd also like to recommend my book encouraging an experimental approach to prayer: *The Little Book of Prayer Experiments* (SPCK, 2016).

The books by Marcus J. Borg and John Dominic Crossan are a good place to start if you are interested in the historical–critical tradition of biblical interpretation. They are very readable explorations of how knowing more about the historic context of events, and historical forms and genres, can shed new light and give new depth to our reading of the biblical accounts: *The First Christmas: What the Gospels Really Teach About Jesus's Birth* (SPCK, 2008) and *The Last Week: What the Gospels Really Teach About Jesus's Final Days in Jerusalem* (SPCK, 2008).

I'd also highly recommend Peterson Toscano's 'Transfigurations' DVD/YouTube videos, for a great introduction to queer biblical scholarship. I first saw these performed at Greenbelt (which I also highly recommend as a good place to explore your faith!) and have since used the DVD in church Bible studies. See https://petersontoscano.com/transfigurations/ for more details.

A book I've particularly enjoyed recently on feminist readings of the Old Testament is Wilda C. Gafney's *Womanist Midrash: A Reintroduction to the Women of the Torah and the Throne* (Westminster John Knox Press, 2017).

A more challenging long read, but highly recommended if you would like to go deeper into this subject, is John Barton's *A History of the Bible: The Book and Its Faiths* (Allen Lane, 2019). Academic introductory textbooks that give an overview of a particular area are also a good place to go if you would like to explore a specific topic in more depth; see, for example, *Black Theology* by Anthony G. Reddie (SCM, 2012) and *The Oxford Handbook of Feminist Theology*, edited by Mary McClintock Fulkerson and Sheila Briggs (OUP, 2014).

HODDER &
STOUGHTON

Hodder & Stoughton is the UK's
leading Christian publisher,
with a wide range of books from
the bestselling authors in the UK
and around the world ranging from
Christian lifestyle and theology to
apologetics, testimony and fiction.
We also publish the world's
most popular Bible translation
in modern English, the New
International Version, renowned
for its accuracy and readability.

Hodderfaith.com   Hodderbibles.co.uk
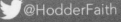@HodderFaith   /HodderFaith